501 Ways
to Use
the Overhead Projector

TO USE
THE OVERHEAD PROJECTOR

Lee Green

Professor
University of Northern Colorado

Illustrated by

Don Dengerink

1982
LIBRARIES UNLIMITED, INC.
Littleton, Colorado

Copyright © 1982 Libraries Unlimited, Inc.
All Rights Reserved
Printed in the United States of America

LIBRARIES UNLIMITED, INC.
P.O. Box 6633
Englewood, CO 80155-6633
1-800-237-6124

Library of Congress Cataloging in Publication Data

Green, Lee.
    501 ways to use the overhead projector.

    Bibliography: p. 111
    1. Overhead projection--Handbooks, manuals, etc. 2. Education, Elementary--Curricula--Audio-visual aids--Handbooks, manuals, etc. I. Title.
II. Title: Five hundred one ways to use the over-head projector.
LB1043.5.G733   1982   371.3'35   82-13025
ISBN 0-87287-339-0

Parts of this book are based on *Use Your Overhead*, by Lee Green (Wheaton, IL: Victor Books), © 1979 by SP Publications, Inc.

Table of Contents

Introduction to the Overhead Projector

Of all projection equipment, the overhead projector lends itself most to meeting the communication needs of the individual classroom teacher. It was developed during World War II to facilitate the training of servicemen and is one of the few pieces of audiovisual equipment designed specifically for classroom use. Its great flexibility, ease of operation, and inexpensive materials make the overhead one of the greatest tools ever designed for the teaching profession.

**This here overhead projector was created during World War II it taught me everything I needed to know...
well, almost everything...**

The overhead projector began to be widely used in the public schools of the United States in the late 1950s and early 1960s. At first, few teachers understood how to utilize the overhead. Most teachers—for fear of failure or lack of information—avoided using the overhead at all. During the past 30 years, a vast number of creative applications and techniques have been developed. This book is designed to stimulate your creative thinking and to help you better utilize the overhead in your classroom. Overhead utilization is limited only by your imagination.

IMAGE MANIPULATION

The overhead has been called the flannelboard of the projected media. The large horizontal stage permits materials to be laid down and manipulated. Image manipulation capability gives the overhead a flexibility not found in other projection equipment. Information may be progressively revealed by laying objects on the stage; marking, writing, or shading; uncovering cardboard masks; or laying additional sheets of plastic over the base transparency.

The Flannelboard of Projected Media...

By just moving these...

VISUALIZING RELATIONSHIPS

The second, most singular advantage of the overhead is its ability to visualize relationships. Because visuals may be quickly and cheaply produced, no other audiovisual tool can visualize relationships more effectively than the overhead. Specific ideas and applications will be presented in later chapters; however, here are some general applications:

1. **IDEA RELATIONSHIPS**

    The relationship of main ideas in a speech, lesson, or unit of study can be introduced or reviewed on the overhead.

2. **STATISTICAL RELATIONSHIPS**

    Line graphs, pie charts, and bar graphs quickly visualize the relationship of statistical data. Visualizing data assists the learner to grasp quickly the significance of the data.

3. **SPACIAL RELATIONSHIPS**

    Size, shape, distance, and area relationships can be quickly grasped through the use of various maps and organizational charts. For example, the relative size of one country to another can be shown by making a base transparency and an overlay.

4. **TEMPORAL RELATIONSHIPS**

    Events in other parts of the world contemporary with the American Revolution can be visualized with a time line. Various graphs and charts can assist the learner in perceiving the interrelationships of historical events.

5. **COMPONENT RELATIONSHIPS**

    A cut-away drawing of a piece of machinery can quickly visualize the function and relationship of component parts of the machine and how it operates. Relationships of parts of the human body may also be visualized.

6. **STRUCTURAL RELATIONSHIPS**

    The structure of language can be quickly visualized with the overhead. Verb conjugations, tenses, adjective placement, and other structural relationships may be quickly perceived through use of the overhead.

STRUCTURE OF THE OVERHEAD PROJECTOR

Another major advantage of the overhead is its ease of operation. There are no sprocket holes or threading patterns to cause worry. The overhead projector is a simple, light box in which a projection lamp beams light through a magnifying lens, via a mirror, onto a screen.

A brilliant projection lamp allows the projector to be used in a well-lighted room. The large aperture (window through which light passes) is 10x10 inches or larger. A larger aperture results in a large image on the screen when the projector is placed a short distance from the screen. The overhead projector is operated in front of the class rather than at the back of the room, as is done with 16mm and filmstrip projectors. Thus, the teacher faces the audience and maintains eye contact.

OVERHEAD TRANSPARENCY TERMINOLOGY

Understanding a few basic terms is helpful in utilizing the overhead projector. Here is some of the basic vocabulary used with transparencies:

1. **APERTURE:**

    This is the window in a transparency mount—the area through which light passes and is thus projected onto the screen.

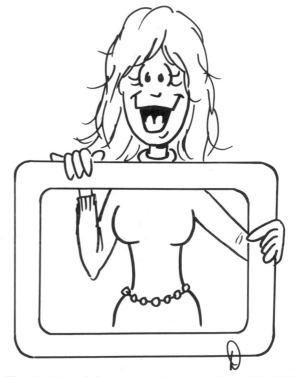

The inside of the mount is called the APERTURE.

2. **BASE CELL:**

    This is the basic transparency that is mounted to the back of a transparency frame. A base cell may be composed of several sheets of acetate, sandwiched and taped together. Any and all sheets taped to the back of the frame are considered a base cell. Cell is sometimes spelled "Cel" to distinguish it from other types of cells.

3. **OVERLAY:**

Acetate sheets taped to the front of the mount and then laid over the base cell are called overlays. A transparency may have multiple overlays:

a. **Fixed Sequence:** A fixed sequence results when all the overlays are taped to a single edge of the overhead transparency frame.

b. **Random Sequence:** To have a random sequence, each overlay must be taped to a different edge of the transparency frame. Thus, overlays may be laid over the base cell in a variety of sequences.

4. **MASK:**

Cardboard or opaque paper taped to the front of a transparency frame is called a mask. There are different kinds of masks. Further information on masks is presented in chapter 9.

In summary, the following are the chief advantages and disadvantages of the overhead projector:

ADVANTAGES

1. The overhead is simple to operate.

2. Teacher- or student-made material can be designed to meet local classroom needs.

3. Up-to-date materials, such as material from the daily newspaper, can be quickly and economically produced for classroom use.

4. An instructor can save much time over chalkboard utilization by preparing materials ahead of time. He or she may use transparencies for quick reference or review.

5. The instructor is in control of the pace of the presentation. He or she may gear the pace to the response of the students.

6. Large image size allows for image manipulation, such as marking, masking, and overlaying. The overhead is conducive to student use.

7. Sets of transparencies may be stored in a small space and quickly retrieved. (Chapter 10 presents storage and retrieval ideas.)

8. Overhead transparencies may be used with other media. Overhead/audiotape presentations, much like slide/tape presentations, may be produced by teachers or students. An overhead transparency that presents the structure of a machine or composition of a painting may be projected alongside a 35mm slide.

9. Many commercial companies produce high-quality, low-cost overhead transparencies in most discipline areas. Check with a local audiovisual dealer for a catalogue.

DISADVANTAGES

1. Instructors often exhibit poor presentation techniques when using the overhead. (Chapter 2 presents good utilization techniques.)

2. Quick, low-cost production often results in poor-quality transparencies. There is a temptation to type 150 or more words on a page and to make a heat copy transparency.

3. Instructors often place too much copy on a single transparency. Transparencies are sometimes used instead of a handout. Overhead transparencies may be used to explain a handout, but should not be used in lieu of a handout.

4. The advantage of eye contact is often destroyed by poor presentation techniques. Instructors often read material off the screen or leave the projector turned on after the visual has been removed, thus blinding the audience.

5. The overhead does not replace a 35mm slide. Photographic reality is possible, but generally costly. Halftone reproduction is often difficult. Color is usually added mechanically. A 35mm slide made on the copy stand may be better for a given situation than an overhead transparency.

TYPES OF OVERHEAD TRANSPARENCIES

There are four families of materials which may be used on the overhead projector: 1) Realia (real objects); 2) Handmade materials; 3) Machine-made materials; and 4) Photographic transparencies. A chapter about each type of material is presented in this book.

SUMMARY

This chapter states that the overhead projector is one of the most flexible teaching tools available. Some of its chief advantages are image manipulation, the ability to visualize relationships, and the ability to produce, cheaply and locally, materials tied to the curriculum. It has also been noted that low-cost, quick, local production, and ease of operation sometimes results in shoddy, poorly designed transparencies and poor presentation techniques. The next several chapters deal with correct presentation techniques, transparency design, and utilization ideas.

Utilization Techniques

Poorly designed and utilized transparencies can negate many of the advantages of the overhead projector. Chapters 2 and 3 present ideas to help you improve your presentation effectiveness.

SCREEN PLACEMENT

TRIPOD SCREEN

Nothing is more disconcerting than to be a member of an audience and to not be able to see visuals as they are projected on a screen. If the screen is placed front and center of the audience, the presenter often blocks the view of the audience. To avoid this, the screen should be placed in one corner of the room at an angle so that every person can see it.

WALL SCREENS

A large wall screen should be hung high enough on the wall for the whole audience to view. If the ceiling is low, hang the screen at an angle in one corner to permit everyone a view. To eliminate keystoning, hang the screen away from the wall so the bottom may be tied back. (For further information, see Keystoning in this chapter.)

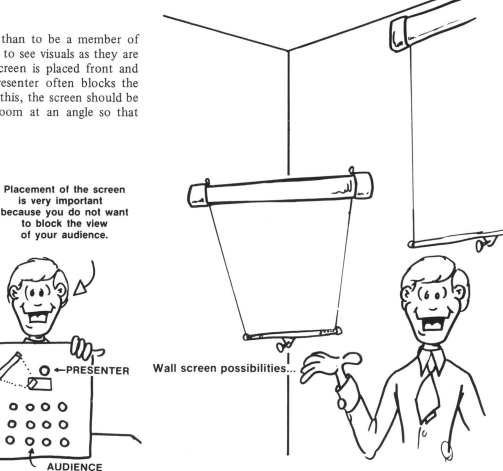

DON'T OBSTRUCT THE VIEW

Placement of the screen is very important because you do not want to block the view of your audience.

←PRESENTER

AUDIENCE

Wall screen possibilities...

FLAT, WHITE WALL SURFACES

A screen should be no smaller than 50x50 inches for general classroom use. A 60x60-inch screen is even better. If a large screen is not available, it may be better to project onto a large, light-colored wall surface if it is available. Remember that the image should be large enough for the person in the back row to read.

I just created a masterpiece...it's a wall screen.

FLAT WHITE

KEYSTONING

Keystoning is a fan-shaped image resulting from unequal distance from the projector lens to the top and bottom of the screen. Keystoning results if the screen is placed much higher than the projector lens. Keystoning may be eliminated by slanting the top of the screen forward, or the bottom backward, to equalize the distance to the projector lens. Tripod screens may be purchased with an attachment or arm that allows the screen to be slanted forward at the top. This is called a "keystone eliminator." Wall screens should be mounted two or more feet away from the wall so they may be slanted back at the bottom to eliminate keystoning. Horizontal keystoning may also result from not placing the projector squarely in front of the screen.

Keystone Eliminator

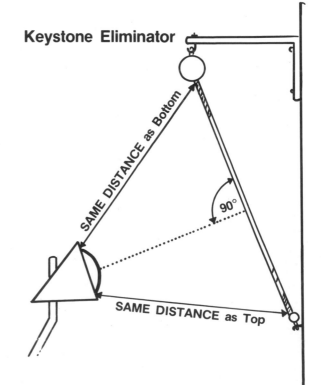

DETERMINING SCREEN SIZE

Audience size and room shape should be considered when determining the correct screen size. Projected transparencies must be readable to the person farthest from the screen. Use the *Rule of 6* to determine screen size. Measure the distance from the screen to the person farthest away; divide the distance by six for the minimum screen size. For example, if the distance to the back row is 60 feet, divide 60 by 6 for the correct screen size—10 feet. This is the screen width. However, no screen smaller than 60x60 inches should be used with the overhead.

REAR PROJECTION SCREENS

Commercially produced rear projection screens are quite expensive. You can make your own rear projection screen by constructing a wooden frame and stretching frosted acetate, or an unpatterned frosted shower curtain, over it. Frosted acetate is obtainable in rolls of various widths. Larger screens can be made from the translucent plastic shower curtain. Stretch the plastic over a framework constructed of 1x3-inch lumber. Rear projection screens permit much student involvement, such as touching or pointing to objects projected onto the screen.

To figure screen size:
÷ the distance to the farthest viewer by 6
= the size of the screen you need...

THE RIGHT SCREEN SURFACE

Wall and tripod screens are marketed with three types of surface: mat, silver/aluminum, and beaded. Silver and beaded screens are used largely for motion picture projection. The mat surface screen is best for overhead projection. A screen may be constructed of plywood or masonite and painted with flat white paint. Homemade screens should, however, be hung to eliminate keystoning.

KEEPING THE PROJECTOR CLEAN

Because there are many different models of overhead projectors, it is difficult to give specific instructions on cleaning them. In some cases, cleaning may entail dismantling the projector. Dirt on the lens or projector stage results in dirty smudges on the screen, and cuts light output. Do *not* use household glass cleaners on the lens or stage of the overhead; these cleaning agents leave a film. Use a liquid camera lens cleaner on all glass surfaces of the overhead projector. (The cleaner is available in pint cans at local photo stores.) Avoid using rags having lint. You may have to remove the protective glass over the Fresnel lens and clean both sides.

HOW TO IMPROVE
YOUR OVERHEAD PRESENTATIONS

Making a presentation on the overhead projector is not difficult, but it does take a little practice and requires some helpful tips. Here are a few of the Do's and Don'ts of overhead projection:

1. **DO**   Keep your transparencies simple.

   DON'T   Have more than 8 to 10 lines of type or intricate, complex drawings.

2. **DO**   Use large, easy-to-read type.

   DON'T   Use an elite or pica typewriter to type out long messages for a heat copy transparency.

3. **DO**   Maintain eye contact with your audience.

   DON'T   Read material from the screen or turn your back to the audience.

4. **DO**   Run a focus check on your first transparency.

   DON'T   Continue your presentation before checking the screen to see if the first transparency is in focus.

5. **DO**   Check to see if the transparency is positioned squarely on the screen.

   DON'T   Depend on the audience to tell you if the visual is crooked on the screen.

6. **DO**   Turn off the projector when changing transparencies or when you are through talking about the transparency. This allows the audience's attention to return to you.

   DON'T   Blind your audience by leaving the projector on without an image on it.

7. **DO**   Sit or stand beside the projector.

   DON'T   Pace about the room while the transparency is being projected—this can be very distracting.

8. **DO**   Make sure each member of the audience can see the screen.

   DON'T   Place the screen so that you block the view of someone in the audience.

9. **DO**   Make sure the screen is large enough for transparencies to be easily read by those in the back row.

   DON'T   Forget to use the *Rule of 6* in determining the correct screen size.

10. **DO**   Use a handout to explain in detail the information you wish to present. Use the overhead to present key ideas.

   DON'T   Place more than 25 to 30 words on a transparency. Consider a series of transparencies if more are necessary.

Often, we cannot be objective in judging ourselves. It is a good idea to have a sympathetic friend sit in the last row of the audience and critique your presentation. The following 10-point checklist was developed to help you evaluate your presentation:

TEN-POINT EVALUATION SHEET

GOOD   NEEDS IMPROVING

1. ____ ____ Was the screen size adequate so viewers in the back row could easily read the transparencies?

2. ____ ____ Was the screen positioned so everyone in the audience could see it, or did the presenter block the audience's view?

3. ____ ____ Were the transparencies in focus? Did the presenter check to see if they were focused properly?

4. ____ ____ Were the transparencies positioned correctly on the screen, or were they crooked? Did the presenter check to see if they were correctly positioned so as to not run off the screen?

5. ____ ____ Were the transparencies simple and easy to read—not having too much or too complex of material?

6. ____ ____ Was the lettering large enough to be read easily?

7. ____ ____ Did the presenter turn off the projector at the appropriate time, such as between transparencies? Were you distracted by the glare from a blank screen?

GOOD   NEEDS IMPROVING

8. ____ ____ Did the presenter maintain eye contact with the audience, or did he/she read material from the screen?

9. ____ ____ Did the presenter leave a transparency on the projector so long that it became distracting or boring?

10. ____ ____ Did the presenter use a pointer or pencil to point out information? Did he/she manipulate overlays or masks skillfully? If not, what suggestions do you have for improvement?

Further Comments:

SUMMARY

The flexibility of the overhead projector may encourage distracting presentation techniques. It is important to have the correct screen size, placed so that the entire audience can view it. A dirty projector detracts from an otherwise quality presentation. A sympathetic friend can be most helpful in assisting you to improve your presentation skills. If available, use a video tape recorder to record your presentation, and then sit down and critically view the tape. Using the overhead requires skill that can be developed only by practice. Don't be afraid to try new techniques—that's how overhead utilization techniques were born. Vary the type of transparencies, and use color to brighten them. An overhead presentation can become very boring if all the transparencies are the same. The next chapter presents ideas for good overhead transparency design.

How to Design a Good Overhead Transparency

The feel for design, perhaps, is caught and not taught. Some people have a talent for design; others do not. Some people doubt that graphic design can be taught to everyone. However, it is the opinion of this author that anyone can produce a readable transparency by following a few guidelines. Imitation and practice are the best ways to develop graphic design skills. This chapter presents some basic guidelines for overhead transparency design.

GRAPHIC DESIGN IMITATION

An excellent way to develop graphic skills is to imitate professional artwork found in brochures, magazine layouts, newspaper advertisements, and posters. Study how the artist uses color, type style and size, line, and texture to communicate the message. Try to isolate some key ideas, and seek to incorporate them into your own designs. Professional artists often get ideas from each other and use them in their own artwork. Develop a file of graphic layout and design ideas. You may want to classify them under use of line, type, composition, and color.

LAYOUT SHEETS

The use of a grid sheet having 1/4-inch squares is most helpful in overhead transparency design. Blue-line grid sheets are available at office supply or graphic arts stores. Grid sheets will help keep lettering of uniform height and from running downhill. It is easy to vary lettering size by making the lettering 1, 2, or 3 squares high. For text-type transparencies, try making the heading 3 or 4 squares high, main points 2 squares high, and subpoints 1 square high. Headings are generally all capital letters, and main points and text lower-case. An additional help is to place a transparency mount over the grid sheet and, in blue pencil, trace around the aperture. This will visualize the area to be utilized in a mounted transparency. Without this, the tendency is to run the material out beyond the 7½x9½-inch area of the transparency mount so that the material on the transparency is too large to use a transparency mount. The general rule is not to place transparency artwork closer than ½ inch from the edge of the 7½x9½-inch aperture of the transparency mount. Placing material close to the edge of the transparency mount results in the mounted transparency looking too crowded. The layout sheet with a line outlining the aperture of the transparency mount will help you visualize how the transparency will look when mounted.

Make your own layout sheet

THE KISS METHOD

The first rule of overhead transparency design is simply *KISS*—Keep It Simple, Stupid; put another way, "Think Coloring Book."

Use simple line drawings and bold, simple lettering for maximum readability. Coloring books have simple line drawings made with bold, heavy lines. Involved and intricate drawings, charts, or maps confuse the audience. Complex or involved ideas often can be simplified and made into a series of transparencies rather than a single one. Cartoons, simple outline maps, pen and ink sketches, and line illustrations are best. Simple, high-contrast half-tones may be reproduced on certain heat copy materials. A further discussion of this appears in chapter 7.

TWELVE GUIDELINES

Here are 12 guidelines to assist you in improving overhead transparency designs:

1. *Use Simple Block Lettering.* Use bold lettering, such as Gothic. Study newspaper headlines and headings—they leap out at you. Avoid tall, thin, ornate, or flowery lettering. No lettering should be smaller than ¼ inch. NEVER type 100 or more words with pica or elite type to produce a heat copy transparency master. If you type a master, use a large type typewriter, such as a primary or bulletin board typewriter. See chapter 5 for hand-lettering ideas and techniques.

2. *Vary the Size of the Type.* A mistake often made in transparency design is to make all lettering the same size. Develop dominance and subordination through the use of type. It is a good idea to place a title or heading at the top of a text-type transparency. A heading orients the audience to the idea or concept you will present in the transparency. Headings should be bold and usually in all capital letters. See the material under Layout Sheets in this chapter. Main points should have smaller type and may be lower case. Subpoints should be subordinated by using smaller type than the main points. Place a symbol or asterisk before points of

equal value to give them unity. For example, if there are four subpoints under a main point, unify these four points by placing a dot, square, star, or asterisk before each of the four points.

3. *Use Lines to Draw Attention.* Graphic artists often use one line to set off a caption or key idea. A heading may be set off by placing a line under it, thus separating it from the text. A line above and below a heading will further set it off. A heading may also be enclosed within an oval or rectangle. A box may be used to unify and set off a group of related ideas. Further information is presented under formats for overhead transparency design.

4. *Avoid Vertical Compositions.* Screens generally are rectangular—wider than they are tall. Thus, a vertical overhead transparency bleeds off the top and bottom of the screen. To compensate for this, the projector must be moved closer to the screen, thereby reducing letter size and readability of the transparency. A good rule is to avoid vertical overhead transparencies.

5. *Avoid Vertical Lettering.* While this rule will not always hold, it is better to avoid vertical lettering. We have been taught to read horizontally from left to right. Vertical lettering generally hinders readability.

6. *Placement of Caption.* While not a hard and fast rule, we generally begin reading at the upper left-hand corner of a book; thus, the upper left-hand corner is a prime spot to place a caption. We also generally look for a caption beneath a cartoon or illustration. Therefore, if there is an illustration on the transparency, the audience will look at the upper left-hand corner or beneath the drawing for the caption.

7. *Rule of Thirds.* Generally avoid placing a drawing in the center of a composition. Use a blue pencil and make light pencil lines to divide the layout sheet into thirds, both vertically and horizontally. Where the vertical and horizontal lines intersect (four spots) is a good place to locate a drawing. This also leaves ample space for a good-sized caption and will result in an informal balance composition.

LAW of THIRDS

8. *Formal and Informal Balance.* If used too much, formal balance becomes monotonous. Formal balance is like dividing a composition in the middle with an imaginary line. What is placed on one side

must also be placed on the other. It is like a teeter-totter balanced on both sides by two people the same size.

FORMAL BALANCE

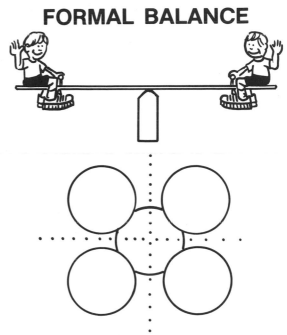

In informal balance, the fulcrum of the teeter-totter is placed some place other than the center of the composition. Just as a small child may balance a heavier adult by placing the fulcrum closer to the heavier adult, so larger figures in a composition may be balanced by smaller ones. There are an infinite number of possible arrangements in informal composition. Use a scratch sheet of paper and a pencil to sketch ideas or cut out shapes from construction paper; move the figures around until a pleasing arrangement is attained. A good way to learn informal balance is to imitate graphic layouts from publications that are pleasing.

INFORMAL BALANCE

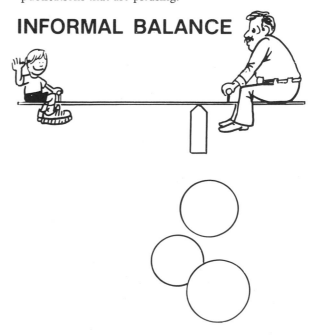

9. *Create a Feeling of Unity.* Place figures or groupings of type so that there is more space outside (between the figure and the transparency frame) than inside or between the figures. An art principle is that broken or intersecting lines unify a design. For example, when using geometric forms such as ovals, circles, or rectangles to enclose ideas, overlap them so that lines intersect. The geometric form will then appear as a whole rather than 3 or 4 separate elements. (See illustration.)

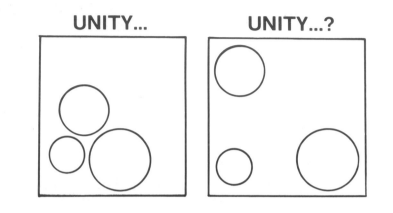

10. *Figure Placement.* When a face or figure is used in an overhead composition, it is best to have the figure looking into the composition rather than away from it. If the figure is to appear as if walking, have it walking into the picture rather than out. You can draw attention to a caption by having a figure looking into the picture towards the caption. Do not make figures too large so as to seem crowded; give them breathing room.

FIGURE PLACEMENT

Figures should be placed so that they are looking at or toward the copy. The reason for this is that the figure catches our attention first and we tend to look at what the figure is looking at...

11. *Amount of Lettering in a Transparency.* When designing a transparency having mostly type, generally limit your copy to 6 to 8 words per line. Limit the lines of type to 8 or 10 when developing a series of statements or points. If your transparency has more than 25 to 30 words on it you are crowding it (or using lettering too small), and you should consider making two or more transparencies in a series.

AMOUNT of LETTERING per transparency

6 to 8 Words per line . . .

WORDS, WORDS, WORDS, WORDS, WORDS, WORDS

WORDS. WORDS. WORDS. WORDS. WORDS. WORDS. WORD

8 to 10 Lines per transparency

Eight to ten lines per transparency.

8 to 10 Lines per Transparency.

Eight to Ten LINES per TRANSPARENCY.

EIGHT TO TEN LINES PER TRANSPARENCY.

6 to 8 Words per Line.

12. *Use Color for Punch.* An art rule is: You add by subtraction. Another way of stating it is: Use color sparingly for a purpose. Use color to draw attention to the center of interest or a heading. Too much color can bring confusion. Use color to unify or highlight what you want the audience to see.

COLOR... REAL PUNCH

FORMATS FOR
OVERHEAD TRANSPARENCY DESIGN

It is difficult for beginners to understand how to use line and geometric form in the design of overhead transparencies. Here are a few ideas.

SINGLE IDEA OR QUOTE

The mounted transparency has a message area of approximately 7½x9½ inches. A single saying or quote may take up only a small part of this area. Line and geometric form are needed to give punch and emphasis to your message. An excellent technique to use is called "billboarding." Your message is enclosed in a rectangle, circle, or oval. These may be made by tracing them with a plastic template available at graphic arts stores. After the message is printed or run onto heat copy transparency material, a sheet of colored acetate is placed over it. Using the outlines of the ovals and circles as a guideline, cut out the circle or oval. Discard the cut-out piece. This leaves the message area in clear (white) and the surrounding area in color. The white area will draw the eye to your message. A simple way to also accomplish the same effect is to cut two or more strips of colored acetate. Mount them above or below the message or four pieces on all four sides of the message. This will result in billboarding but eliminates the tedious task of cutting out circles. Tape the acetate strips to the back of the transparency mount. The message may also be enclosed in a star burst or other geometric form and billboarded with a colored sheet of acetate.

STRIPS OVERLAPPED AT CORNERS

MESSAGE

ACETATE STRIPS

MESSAGE

MESSAGE

MESSAGE

MESSAGE

MESSAGE

COLORED ACETATE

HEADINGS

It is a good idea to use headings on text-type transparencies to orient your audience to your subject. The heading should have the largest and boldest type on the transparency. It may be set off from the text or message by the use of geometric form or line.

THREE-POINT MESSAGE

There are several possible layouts for messages having three points. Start with a heading to direct the audience's thinking on the subject; then draw either two vertical or horizontal lines to divide the message area into three rectangles. Thus, the audience understands that whatever is inside each rectangle is a single thought or idea.

TWO-POINT OR CONTRAST MESSAGE

This message format works well when presenting contrasting ideas. These may be called "Do's and Don'ts" or a "Positive and Negative." Set off the heading with a line and then drop a line down the center of the message area. This separates each idea and gives unity to each contrasting idea.

FOUR-POINT MESSAGE

A four-point message may be organized by making a horizontal and a vertical line in the center of the message area. You may also give all the points a feeling of unity by placing a geometric form in front of each point.

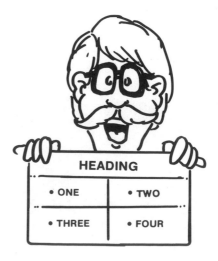

EVALUATING YOUR TRANSPARENCIES

A good way to evaluate a transparency is to project it. This will show inadequacies and flaws that cannot be seen by just looking at it. Apply the *Rule of 6* when evaluating a transparency. The *Rule of 6* is: A visual should be readily readable when viewed from a distance six times the width of the projected image. For example, if a transparency is projected so that it fills a 60x60-inch screen, multiply 60 inches (5 feet) by 6 = 30 feet. View the transparency from 30 feet. Ask yourself the following questions:

1. Is the type large enough? Can the captions be read easily?

2. What do I see first? What is the center of interest?

3. Where does my eye move to next? Does the composition flow?

4. Is the composition simple and clear? Will the audience get the message I want to communicate?

5. Does the composition bother me? Does it seem complete and balanced?

SUMMARY

The primary function of an overhead transparency is to communicate. Slick, arty designs don't necessarily ensure good communication. A crude, simple design may be very readable and superior to artier ones. An overhead transparency should be designed to communicate a single concept or idea. The most common misuse of the overhead is placing too much copy on a single transparency. Typing 100 or more words on a master is a gross misuse. Good overhead design comes from experience. You will see improvement as you produce more and more transparencies. Much can be learned from imitating good graphic design.

Using Realia on the Overhead Projector

The overhead projector's horizontal design facilitates use of realia. Realia is a term often used to denote three-dimensional objects. Opaque objects project as black silhouttes, whereas transparent objects, such as test tubes, petri dishes, and Plexiglas toys, are enlarged for group viewing. One is limited only by one's creative insights. This chapter presents a number of ideas for using realia.

ART

1. When describing different kinds of brushes, place actual brushes on the stage of an overhead. The class will be able to see the size, shape, and texture of the brushes.

Notice the difference in these brushes...

2. Manipulate string or yarn on the stage of the projector to create designs and teach concepts of space division.

3. Use heavy sheets of colored acetate to visualize the mixing of colors (for example, primary and secondary, i.e. yellow and blue make green).

4. An idea similar to that expressed above is to use petri dishes and food coloring in water to show the mixing of secondary colors.

A little food coloring... it's MAGIC!

5. Teach perspective by cutting out identical human or geometric shapes of graduating size. Manipulate them on the overhead stage to show how size gives the illusion of space and perspective.

6. Use paper strips ¼ inch wide to visualize concepts of symmetry and space division by laying them on the projector stage.

7. Use the overhead as a spotlight for lighting still lifes for painting and drawing classes.

8. Observational skills may be developed by placing real objects or cut-out shapes on the projector stage. Quickly flick the lamp on and off. Ask children to draw the shape they saw. Compare their drawings with the object or shape.

BUSINESS

9. Make shorthand symbols out of pipe cleaners. Place them on the projector stage for discussion or drill purposes.

LANGUAGE ARTS

10. Use cut-out shapes for a puppet show to be put on by students. Glue popsicle sticks to the cardboard heads or figures for easy manipulation. Backgrounds may be drawn on acetate. Tape record the narration so children can concentrate on puppet manipulation.

Ye ole overhead talkies...

11. Use cardboard shapes to demonstrate the concepts of on, under, into, and the like.

12. Have children manipulate two cut-out figures or faces on the projector, developing a dialogue and, thus, oral expression. You may hinge the jaw of the figure and manipulate it with a piece of a coat hanger.

13. Teach the concepts of transparency, translucency, and opacity by projecting various materials on the projector.

MATH

14. Lay a transparent plastic ruler on the stage of the projector so that the ruler is magnified for children to see. Use the projection to explain inches. Have the students compare the ruler on the screen with their own. Use for drilling in the use of the ruler.

15. Lay two transparent plastic rulers on the overhead, one in inches and the other in metric. Use the projections to compare inches with centimeters.

16. Use cardboard shapes to teach geometric form, such as triangles, rectangles, and parallelograms.

Note the differences in these shapes...

17. Use cut-out shapes of triangles, parallelograms, and rectangles to explain how to find the area of each.

18. Use a cut-out shape of a circle to explain diameter and circumference.

19. Use Quiscenaire rods to demonstrate math values. You may use cut-out cardboard shapes to teach values and visualize simple addition and subtraction.

20. Use cut-out cardboard shapes to teach fractions. Cut a circle or square into fourths or eighths. Manipulate to show 2 x ¼ = ½ or other values.

21. Make a transparent "geo" board using 7 mil plastic, such as cleared X-ray film. Use paper fasteners inserted into holes punched into the plastic. Cut ends off paper fasteners so that they don't stick out beyond the head of the fastener. Use a nail to punch 42 to 49 points approximately ¾ inches apart. Use rubber bands to demonstrate geometric forms.

22. Use paper clips, beans, or buttons to teach set theory. Cut circles or squares in a sheet of cardboard and use to group objects into sets.

23. Use cardboard shapes of various sizes to teach the concepts of "larger than" and "smaller than."

24. Use buttons, beans, or seeds to visualize the concepts of addition, subtraction, and multiplication.

25. Place an abacus on the stage of the projector to show its use and place values.

26. Demonstrate how to make change by using real coins on the projector stage, or use cut-out shapes the size of coins.

P. E. AND HEALTH EDUCATION

27. Visualize concepts of pedestrian safety or bike safety using cut-out paper shapes to represent students and cars. On a transparency of an intersection or a map, manipulate the shapes to show possible local hazards.

28. Use cut-out paper shapes of stop and regulatory signs to drill students or student drivers on the meaning of sign shapes.

29. Use cut-out shapes, such as squares and circles, to demonstrate basketball plays. Manipulate the cut-outs on a transparency diagram of a basketball court.

30. Manipulate circles and squares to visualize football plays. Manipulate figures on a transparency drawing of a football field. Use to explain skills and rules.

31. In Drivers' Education, use a toy car on a transparency map showing an intersection, a four-lane highway, or other roadways. Manipulate the cars to demonstrate correct traffic procedures.

PHOTOGRAPHY

32. Lay a lens of a view camera on the stage of the overhead projector to visualize stops and shutter speeds to a class.

SCIENCE

33. Lay small leaves on the projector stage to discuss leaf shapes and tree identification. You may place the leaf into an envelope of two heavy sheets of acetate, taped together to preserve the leaf, for future use. Tape the leaf to one sheet of plastic, using double-edged tape.

34. Punch holes into a sheet of cardboard to form a solar system. Project onto the ceiling, and use to teach an astronomy lesson.

35. Make cut-out cardboard shapes of weather symbols. Manipulate the symbols on a map transparency to show how a weather front develops and moves.

36. Demonstrate gear ratio by using a set of gears mounted onto a sheet of Plexiglas. You may cut out a set of cardboard gears, and mount on 7 mil acetate. Fasten the gears to the plastic with a paper fastener.

37. Place iron filings into a transparent plastic envelope made by taping two sheets of 7 mil acetate together. Use a magnet to demonstrate attraction.

Notice how these iron particles are attracted to this magnet . . .

38. Use the overhead as an image magnifier to project crystalline growth in a petri dish.

39. Use a pencil with an eraser and manipulate transparent colored disks to demonstrate the exchange of atoms in reversible equations.

40. Use surplus X-rays to visualize body structure, bones of the body, and their functions.

41. Place a clear Plexiglas directional compass on the projector stage to demonstrate how a compass is used to find directions.

42. Place insects or bugs into petri dishes so that the class can study their movements. Slices from cardboard tubing may be used to enclose insects for study. Place on the projector stage.

43. Illustrate wave motion of sound by placing a tuning fork in a petri dish with a thin layer of colored water in it.

44. Lay a Plexiglas slide rule onto the projector stage. Manipulate the rule to demonstrate its use.

45. Demonstrate chemical reactions by simultaneously placing small strips of aluminum in three petri dishes. One dish should contain hydrochloric acid; one, sodium hydroxide; and the third, nitric acid. Students can observe the reactions.

46. Demonstrate the use of a micrometer or vernier calipers by placing them on the projector stage so that the image is magnified for the class to see.

47. Demonstrate the differences between opacity, translucency, and transparency by placing examples of each on the projector stage.

SOCIAL STUDIES

48. Use cut-out symbols on a background map of a battlefield to visualize the movement of troops in a battle. For example, demonstrate step by step the Battle of Gettysburg.

49. Use cut-out shapes representing various ships of the navy on a background map of an ocean area. Demonstrate a naval battle step by step, such as the Battle of Midway during World War II.

Do you recognize this historic World War II ship?

50. Use cut-out paper shapes of the states to drill in state identification.

SUMMARY

Image manipulation is one of the major advantages of the overhead over other types of projectors. Transparent plastic objects, such as rulers and compasses, may be projected and manipulated. The overhead becomes an image enlarger so that larger audiences may view a process being demonstrated by the teacher. Opaque objects and shapes project as a shadow or black. They, too, may be manipulated to visualize processes. Thus, the overhead has many uses apart from the production of overhead transparencies.

Handmade Transparencies

DETERMINING THE RIGHT PEN

The most important factor in producing handmade transparencies is not the acetate, but the pen. The wrong type of pen will bead up when dry and result in thin, broken lines. There are two types of felt pens: water-soluble and permanent or spirit. Permanent pens are best for making handmade transparencies because they will not smudge when dry.

To determine if the pen you want to use is permanent or water-based:

1. Look at the description on the pen. Sometimes it will state whether it is permanent, smudge-proof, or waterproof.

2. Smell the point. It is a permanent pen if it smells like cleaning fluid.

3. Test the pen on acetate or the palm of your hand. Let a mark dry for 30 seconds. Dampen a finger and try to wipe away the mark. If it is a permanent pen, it will not smudge.

Keep testing pens until you find a brand that will do the job. *Remember that the most important factor in producing traced transparencies is the pen.*

TYPES OF CLEAR PLASTIC

Most types of clear plastic or acetate will work for handmade transparencies. Here are a few:

1. X-ray film. Use either cleared undeveloped X-ray film or developed film that has been immersed in household bleach. Dilute the bleach, using 1 part water to 2 parts bleach. Wash the cleared film in a mild detergent and rinse. Hang to dry on a clothes line. X-ray film is 7 mil acetate and may have a blue tint. It is available at hospitals, clinics, doctors' offices, or X-ray labs.

2. Printer's film. Offset printing film may be treated the same way as X-ray film. Any sheet of film 8x10 or larger is suitable.

3. Construction plastic. Construction plastic is available at lumberyards or hardware stores. It is used to cover materials and equipment at construction sites. It appears milky white on the roll. Cut the plastic into 8½x11-inch sheets, using a paper cutter or scissors. A roll will produce several hundred transparencies. Generally, this film is for student use or transparencies that will not be kept over a period of years.

4.   Freezer wrap. Any of the polyurethane plastics will also work for making transparencies. Freezer wrap, sandwich bags, Saran wrap, and other plastics may be hard to work with, but can be used.

5.   Separator notebook sheets. Acetate sheet protectors for three-ring notebooks, and acetate-type clasp folders for term papers, are excellent for handmade transparencies.

PROCESS FOR
MAKING TRACED TRANSPARENCIES

You may have wanted to use the overhead projector but have felt that transparency material is too costly. You also may feel you do not have the special talent needed to create a quality transparency. However, if you can trace, you can produce an acceptable transparency. You need to know where to find the right type of pen and inexpensive acetate. Artwork for tracing is in abundance, for example:

> Coloring books
> Line drawings from children's books
> Comic strips
> Political cartoons
> Comic books
> Simple outline maps
> Brochures
> Illustrations from textbooks
> Posters
> Newspaper headlines (for lettering)
> Children's magazines
> Atlases
> Newspaper advertising

1.   Select the artwork to be traced. It should be a simple line drawing that is easy to trace (such as from a coloring book).

Use a simple line drawing...

2.   Tacktape the drawing to a smooth surface, such as a table or desk.

3.   Select the acetate, and tacktape it over the drawings so that neither of the two will move during tracing.

STEP 2
Tacktape the drawing down.

STEP 3
Place the acetate over the drawing
& tacktape it down.

4.   Trace the drawing with a black or dark permanent pen. Try to duplicate the line quality of the drawing, making heavy, wide lines where such lines appear in the drawing.

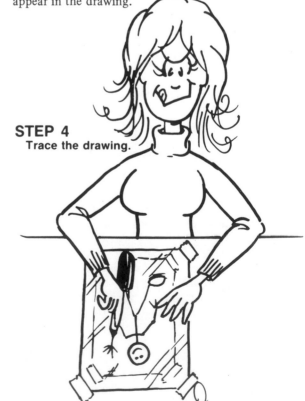

STEP 4
Trace the drawing.

5. When you have completed tracing, remove the acetate from the drawing. Turn the acetate over and add color to the backside. This will prevent smearing.

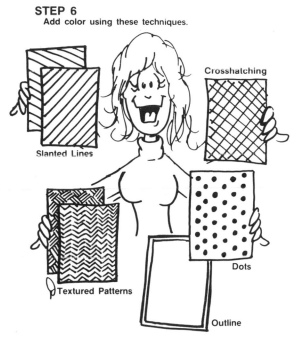

STEP 6
Add color using these techniques.

Slanted Lines

Crosshatching

Textured Patterns

Dots

Outline

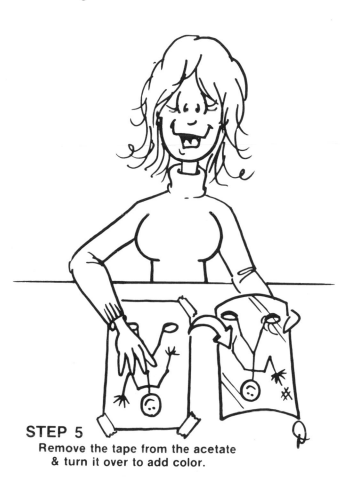

STEP 5
Remove the tape from the acetate & turn it over to add color.

6. Add color with a felt pen. Use the following techniques to add color:

A. Crosshatching

B. Outlining or coloring a line inside the black

C. Making dots

D. Using a yellow pen to add punch to a caption by shading in an area over and around the caption

(When coloring in larger areas of color, use a circular motion with the pen. Do not go over an area more than once. Lighter colors look more pleasing than dark colors, which show up pen strokes more.)

LETTERING AND
GRAPHIC ARTS MATERIALS

A transparency may be composed of only lettering, such as the main points of a lesson, unit of study, or speech. Here are some ideas for making lettering.

1. Newspaper Headlines. Simple, inexpensive lettering guides may be made by clipping letters from newspaper headings and pasting them to a sheet of paper. Arrange the letters in alphabetical order. Use these guides to trace letters onto acetate.

It's a FANTASTIC lettering guide...

NEWSPAPER HEADLINES

2. Stencil Lettering Guides. Stencil lettering guides are inexpensive and may be purchased at office supply stores or discount houses. Trace the letters and fill in the gaps of the stencil letter. Very attractive lettering may be done by using these guides. For further information write to:

> Dennison Manufacturing Co.
> Framingham, MA 01701

I get perfect letters every time with my STENCILS.

3. Dry Transfer Letters. Professional-appearing hand-made transparencies may be produced using dry transfer—sometimes called rub-on lettering. A number of companies, such as Chartpak, Format, Letraset, and Prestype, produce this type of lettering which is available at graphic art or office supply stores. If dry transfer lettering is not available locally, you may obtain information by writing to:

> Prestype, Inc.   Letraset, USA, Inc.
> 194 Veterans Blvd.   33 New Bridge Road
> Carlstadt, NJ   Bergenfield, NJ
> 07072   07621

Dry transfer letters are available in many styles and sizes. Other types of graphic material include: textures, colored lettering, arrows, symbols, border tapes, numerals, and tonal patterns. Because utilization techniques vary slightly depending upon the company manufacturing the lettering material, if you are not familiar with dry transfer lettering, you

should write to one of the companies listed above and ask for a catalogue and other literature presenting application techniques.

It's AMAZING...

Just rub them

4. Hand-Lettering. The lettering quality of hand-lettered transparencies will be greatly improved by following a few graphic arts techniques.

A. Use blue-lined grid paper under a clear sheet of acetate. Grid sheets are available at office supply or graphic art stores. Use the grid lines to make lines of lettering straight and of uniform height. This more than anything else will improve the professional look of your lettering. You may want to print your lettering on the grid sheet with a #2 soft lead pencil, then trace it onto the acetate.

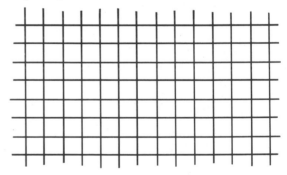

B. DO NOT try to imitate professional lettering, such as newspaper headings. DO NOT use a ruler to make the lettering. Use flowing curved lines to form the letters. Try to make stylized lettering.

LUNCH
Lettering

C. Small lettering may be made by imitating showcard lettering found in the caption balloons of the daily comic strips. Practice until you can do it quickly.

D. Make lettering with pull-down strokes of the pen. You have more control over your hand when pulling down than pushing up.

E. Use lettering size and bulk to emphasize or subordinate ideas. You may emphasize a word by making it larger, boxing it in with lines, or enclosing it in a geometric form.

F. Use all capital letters for headings and main ideas. Use upper- and lower-case letters to subordinate ideas and set them off from headings and main ideas.

G. Reversal-type lettering may be made by drawing a line around the word, phrase, or group of words. Color in the area between the line and outline of the letters. Leave the letters white (clear).

H. All lettering should have good contrast. This may be done by using a dark-colored pen for the lettering or by outlining light-colored lettering with a black or, dark pen. Use splashes of color sparingly, only to highlight a word or meaning. Too much color will confuse the audience as to what is most important and what is less important.

I. A pleasing shadow-lettering effect is obtained by shading in one side of each letter. The lettering appears to have a bright light shining on it from a side direction, thus casting shadows on the other side.

J. By overlapping large outline-type letters, larger and more lettering can be placed in a space.

K. Practice your own style of hand-lettering until you can do it quickly.

5. Color Adhesive Film. Another product that can enhance your handmade transparencies is color adhesive film. It can add color and punch to otherwise dull transparencies. It is sold by most companies marketing dry transfer lettering. If you cannot find this material locally, write to:

> 3M Corporation
> Visual Products Division
> 3M Center
> St. Paul, MN 55101

Step-by-step procedures for using color adhesive film will be presented in chapter 6.

6. Graphic Tapes. Transparent and projectable color tapes are excellent for making bar and line graphs. These materials come in widths 1/32 to 1 inch wide in 11 colors. To create a bar graph, simply roll off the length of material needed, then cut and press the adhesive-backed material to the acetate. If these materials are not available locally, write for a catalogue to:

> Chartpak
> 4 River Road
> Leeds, MA 01053

This PROJECTABLE COLORED TAPE is SUPER. Just peel and stick!

Today's story is about...

7. Die-cut Plastic Letters. Adhesive-backed plastic die-cut letters are available at office supply and discount stores. They are available in various sizes and colors. However, remember they are opaque and will always project as black on the screen. Simply peel off the letters from the backing sheet, and apply to the acetate.

8. Colored Acetate. A quick, inexpensive way to add color and punch to a transparency is to use colored acetate. Colored acetate is available in a number of forms at art stores and office supply stores. Techniques for using colored acetate in transparency design was covered in chapter 3 under Formats for Overhead Transparency Design.

Very professional-appearing transparencies may be produced by people who are not graphic artists by using tracing techniques, rub-on lettering, and graphic materials. To assist you in applying these ideas, here are 60 ideas for producing handmade transparencies. Most of these ideas are elementary level. Secondary level ideas appear in chapter 11.

IDEAS FOR PRODUCING HANDMADE TRANSPARENCIES

LANGUAGE ARTS

1. *Visualize a Story.* Coloring books are inexpensive artwork for illustrating a story. Older children can trace illustrations onto construction plastic to present the story.

2. *Complete a Story.* Use illustrations from children's books or coloring books to trace onto plastic. Illustrate only half the story, stopping at the climax; then ask students to complete the story orally.

3. *Make a Filmstrip.* Read a story to students and ask them to illustrate it using felt pens and construction plastic. You may want to make assignments so that each child illustrates a portion of the story. Pictures may be drawn on an acetate roll and rolled across the stage as the story is told. A roll attachment is probably available for your overhead projector.

4. *Flannelgraph Techniques.* Draw or trace a background scene onto plastic. Use heavy 7 mil acetate, such as X-ray film, cut into strips. Draw or trace a character from the story onto each strip of acetate. Manipulate the characters on the background scene while telling the story.

5. *Key Words*. Write key words and characters from a story on acetate. Use this to review the story. Ask students to tell the story in the proper sequence, using the key words on the transparency.

Today's story is about...

GOOD GUYS

BAD GUYS

6. *Make Up a Story*. Outline a simple plot for a story, giving the character and situation. Ask students to make up a story about this situation and to illustrate it on sandwich bags or freezer wrap. They then tell the story, presenting their illustrations on the overhead projector.

7. *Matching Captions*. The teacher uses handmade transparencies to tell the children a story. Each student is given a word or caption to match each illustration. To review the story, ask students to come and place the correct word or caption on the overhead at the proper point in the story.

8. *Mixed-Up Sequence*. Write out in short sentences the key action phrases from a story. Print these phrases on strips of heavy acetate. Scramble the sequence of ideas, and distribute to students. Ask students to reconstruct the sequence of the story by placing the acetate strips one by one on the projector.

9. *Stick Figures*. Use stick figures on acetate to illustrate a story, a story problem in math, or an event in history. Water-soluble pens will wipe clean with a damp cloth so the acetate may be used repeatedly.

10. *Cartoon Dialogue*. Trace a cartoon strip from a newspaper onto acetate. Eliminate the dialogue of one character, and ask children to write the dialogue representing to that character. To teach the ideas you want, you may make up your own dialogue for the first character.

11. *Picture Dictionary*. Make a picture dictionary of word meanings by tracing illustrations out of books. Workbooks and children's books contain much useful material. Use the projected dictionary to refer to words found in a story.

12. *Word Scramble*. Write words on a sheet of acetate, then scramble the spellings. Make a game of unscrambling the words. You may have two teams; the first team to unscramble the words correctly is the winner.

13. *Book Reports*. Ask students to illustrate their book reports by tracing or drawing them onto plastic. Book jackets may be used as basic artwork for a presentation.

14. *Sharing Poetry*. Ask students to write a poem they have composed onto acetate, and share it with the class. Ask them to share feelings, emotional experiences, or adventures.

15. *Choral Reading*. Place the words to a choral reading on a transparency that will allow students to focus their attention on one point—the screen. Use large, easy-to-read lettering.

16. *Mechanics of Outlining*. Use two overhead projectors. Place a brief passage or paragraph on one projector. Use the second projector to demonstrate how to make an outline of the written passage. Develop it step by step, allowing students to ask questions if they do not understand each step.

17. *Paragraph Formation*. Cut several strips of heavy acetate. Print a complete sentence on each strip. Develop a series of related sentences, or copy a paragraph. Scramble the sentences, then ask students to assemble them to form a paragraph.

MATH

18. *Story Problems*. Trace grocery advertisements to visualize story problems found in the math textbook.

19.   *Manipulative Clock.* With a felt pen, trace around a salad plate onto acetate. Use heavy acetate, such as X-ray film. Write numbers 1 through 12 on the acetate; make cardboard hands and attach to the acetate, using paper fasteners and cardboard circles for washers. Tape over prongs of the fastener. Hands will be movable for drill purposes.

LOOK, the hands move...

20.   *Concepts of Large and Small.* Use tracing techniques to visualize concepts of large-small or progression. Use artwork from magazines, newspapers, and workbooks.

21.   *Practical Math.* Teach addition and change-making by cutting out newspaper advertisements listing prices of toys, clothing, or food. Trace drawings onto plastic, and use as you present problems to students. Ask them to add a grocery bill or make change for a purchase.

22.   *Theorems.* Reinforce the presentation of theorems by writing them out on a clear sheet of acetate. Use a sheet of acetate to visualize the step-by-step solution of a problem.

23.   *Working Equations.* Work out equations step by step on X-ray film. Encourage students to ask questions at each step if they do not understand. Use the transparency to give additional remedial help to students after class or to explain to a student who was absent when the equation was presented.

24.   *Geometric Drawings.* Trace or draw geometric drawings onto plastic. You will save much time (rather than drawing them on the chalkboard) because you can use the drawings to review quickly material that was presented previously. Math books have a wealth of material for tracing.

What is this geometric figure?

25.   *Chalkboard Graphs.* Make transparencies of various bar and line graph structures. Project these onto the chalkboard. Ask students to use the data to plot and fill in the bars or lines. Mistakes can be erased quickly and easily without destroying the graph structure.

26.   *Pie Charts.* Use colored adhesive material to create simple pie charts. Circles may be drawn onto plastic by tracing salad plates or other circular objects. Use to present budgets and expenditures.

27.   *Bar Graphs.* Use Chartpak graphic tapes to create simple bar graphs. Use to explain the function of graphs.

SOCIAL STUDIES

28.   *Historical Event.* Ask students to draw a series of pictures depicting an event in history which they have studied. Ask students to write a script to go

with the transparencies. They may choose to dramatize the event and record it onto a cassette tape. Make the presentation to other classes, parents, and civic organizations.

This is George Washington crossing the Delaware River...

29. *Visualize Spacial Relationships.* Visually show the size relationship between your state and other countries of the world. Trace a country from a globe (to obtain the correct scale) onto acetate. Make an overlay of your state over the other country. Students will see the size relationship easily when the two outline maps are projected one over the other.

30. *Give Students a Concept of Time.* Let 1/16 of an inch represent a year. Use a time line to visualize the length of the student's life, father's life, oldest person in the community, time back to World War II, Civil War, and the like. Let a point represent the present time and work backwards to events in history. Using the 1/16-inch scale, you can visualize approximately 150 years.

31. *Visualize Geneologies.* Using a hand-drawn family tree chart, show the lineage of historical figures and monarchs.

32. *Chalkboard Maps.* Ask students to trace outline maps onto plastic. Project these outline maps onto the chalkboard where they can be traced. Use maps or drawings to speed up chalkboard work.

33. *Wall Maps.* Ask students to trace maps onto acetate. Place onto the overhead projector, and project onto butcher paper tacked to a chalkboard or wall. Trace the enlarged image to create various types of wall maps. Refer to the maps as you teach.

34. *Mural.* Ask students to trace drawings from textbooks, encyclopedias, and other sources onto plastic. Use famous figures, battles, or cultural things such as artificats, dress, or tools. Assemble these drawings into a mural by projecting them onto butcher paper and tracing with felt pens.

35. *Reinforce Names.* When lecturing on major events, administrations, and the history of a country, reinforce hard-to-spell or -pronounce names by writing them on a sheet of acetate and projecting them as you pronounce the words.

SCIENCE

36. *Chemical Formulas.* Progressively write out formulas as you talk. Encourage students to ask questions at each step if they do not understand.

37. *Weather Map.* Use a simple outline map transparency with a series of overlays to explain air fronts, wind movements, and weather symbols. Map material may be obtained from the U.S. Weather Bureau.

GENERAL IDEAS

38. *Library - Story Hour.* Children trace coloring books and children's book illustrations onto plastic. Read or dramatize the story onto a cassette tape. For story hour, assign a student monitor to start the recorder, and place the transparencies on the projector at the proper moment.

39. *Course Objectives.* The teacher uses a felt pen and acetate to write the course objectives while discussing them with students.

40. *Main Points of a Unit of Study.* Use the overhead to present the main points of a unit of study. Use the transparency to review the points at the end of the study.

41. *Field Trip.* Write things students are to look for while on a field trip. The teacher may make a simple map to help orient students to the scene. Use the transparency to make observational or task assignments that students are to carry out during the field trip.

42. *Presenting a 16mm Film.* Use a handmade transparency to introduce a 16mm film to a class. Make viewing assignments on a transparency. Use to lead a discussion after viewing the film.

43. *Vocabulary.* Write vocabulary words used in a 16mm film. Use the transparency to define the words and for review after the picture has been shown.

44. *Quiz.* Use the overhead to present a pop quiz. Write questions on acetate with a permanent pen. Write in correct answers with a water-soluble pen. Wipe clean with a damp cloth. Use for students who need to make up work or for review for students who were absent.

45. *Making Announcements.* Reinforce special announcements in the classroom by writing them on a sheet of acetate.

46. *Birthday Greeting.* For elementary level, have students trace greeting or birthday cards for a birthday party or to project onto the screen to welcome back a student who has been ill.

47. *Welcome a New Student.* Write the name and pertinent information about a new student on a transparency. Use the overhead to introduce the new student.

48. *Primary Colors.* Use circles cut from colored acetate to present primary and secondary colors. Overlap circles to produce secondary colors. Label primary colors by writing on the acetate circles.

49. *Lesson Assignments.* Make lesson assignments clearer by writing them on the overhead projector. This clarifies word meanings, spelling, and due dates of assignments.

50. *Rules of Conduct.* Rules of the classroom or rules of conduct may be reinforced by writing them on the overhead while explaining them. Use for review by writing part of an idea on acetate and asking students to come and complete it.

51. *Bulletin Board Materials.* Trace small line drawings onto acetate, and use the overhead projector to enlarge drawings for use on the bulletin board.

52. *Feeling Activity.* Ask students to portray their feelings by drawing on acetate with a felt pen. Give them free rein to express ideas. Ask students to project their transparencies and explain the feelings they are trying to visualize.

53. *Tic-Tac-Toe Game.* Draw a Tic-tac-toe box on a sheet of acetate. Divide the class into two groups. Use as a review vehicle. Ask questions of each team. If a student gets the correct answer, have him or her, place an *X* or *O* in the box. The team that gets three *X*'s or *O*'s in a row first is the winner.

54. *Fantasia Activity.* Play a musical selection on a record player or tape recorder. Ask students to illustrate the mood of the music. Have them project their transparencies as the music is replayed.

55. *Newspaper Headlines.* Ask students to develop ideas for newspaper headlines for an event in history. Ask them to write the ideas on acetate, including their by-lines, and project the headlines for the class to see.

56. *Stained Glass Windows.* Cut scrap cardboard and colored acetate, or use layers of colored adhesive, to create a stained glass window. Use as a background for a musical program or holiday drama.

57. *Stage Scenery.* Stretch a frosted plastic shower curtain (not having a pattern) over a wooden frame to make a rear projection screen. Project hand-drawn scenes onto the rear projection screen. Use as background scenery for a play. Change scenes by changing transparencies.

58. *Craft Project.* Write the steps of a craft project. Use the transparency to explain the project step by step. Project the transparency for the students to refer to during the work session.

59. *Bicycle Safety*. Draw a diagram of a street intersection on heavy plastic. Cut strips of heavy acetate about 3 inches wide. Trace illustrations of cars and bicycles onto the strips. Drawings from workbooks are helpful. Manipulate cars, people, and the bicycle drawings to dramatize safety hazards and safety procedures.

60. *Video Graphic*. When students are producing a classroom TV project, let them write graphics on plastic. Project the graphics onto the screen, and videotape them. Many creative effects can be done for video programs. Use image manipulation to create a type of animation on the overhead, then videotape it.

These are but a few of the ideas possible for low-cost visualization on the overhead projector. It is hoped that you will try some of these and develop ideas of your own.

SUMMARY

Overhead transparencies need not be expensive. By using inexpensive, clear plastic materials, such as construction plastic, freezer wrap, or sandwich bags, students may use the overhead to present stories, speeches, book reports, and research projects. The most important factor in producing handmade transparencies is the pen. Office supply, graphic arts, and audiovisual stores sell permanent and water-soluble pens suitable for overhead use. Handmade transparencies can approach professional quality by tracing bold, simple line drawings. Students and teachers are limited only by their imaginations.

Color Lift Overhead Transparencies

Color lift is sometimes called contact lifting or picture transfer. It is an inexpensive source of photographic, four-color overhead transparencies. The process requires that the picture be printed on a clay-based paper sometimes called enamel stock. To test whether a picture is clay-based, dampen the tip of the index finger and rub a spot on an unprinted area. A white residue remains on the fingertip if the picture is printed on clay-based paper. *Holiday*, *National Geographic*, and *Time* have been printed on clay-based paper.

A color lift transparency results from laminating a sheet of plastic to the picture. The clay coating on the paper dissolves, when placed in water, leaving the printer's ink affixed to the plastic, thus creating an overhead transparency. Most lamination methods will work, such as:

1. Cold lamination materials, such as adhesive-backed acetates and clear adhesive-backed shelf vinyl (Contact).

2. Hot lamination using laminating film and a dry mount press.

3. Hot lamination machines, such as those made by General Binding Corporation.

COLOR LIFTS USING
ADHESIVE-BACKED PLASTIC

The following procedure is written for adhesive-backed clear shelf vinyl, such as Contact or Marvelon, but may be adapted to other cold lamination materials.

Step One: Laminate the picture. Use the following procedure to attach the adhesive-backed material to the clay-based picture:

1. Work on a clean surface, such as a masonite table top.

1.
**Start with
a clean
area...**

3. Stick the exposed 2-inch strip of the adhesive-backed shelf plastic to a smooth surface, such as the center of the table.

4. Carefully center the picture under the shelf vinyl.

5. Grasp the 2-inch folded-back flap from under the plastic sheet, and slowly peel the backing paper off as you rub the surface of the plastic with your hand. Rub back and forth, smoothing out the plastic as you peel.

6. Peel off all the backing paper while smoothing with your hand. Heat or burnishing will increase the adhesion between the plastic and the picture. A hand iron set at 160° may be used instead of burnishing. Use a protective sheet of paper, and quickly pass the iron over the surface in a circular motion. Try to burnish or affix the plastic so that there are no bubbles. *CAUTION*: Too much heat causes the plastic to bubble.

2. Peel back a 2-inch strip.

2. Peel back a 2-inch strip of the backing sheet on one end of the lamination material. Fold the 2-inch paper flap back against the backside. *NOTE*: To avoid wrinkling or sticking to itself, do not peel the entire backing off the lamination sheet at one time.

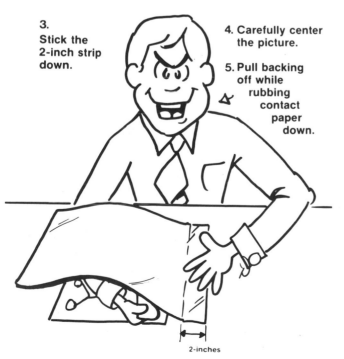

3. Stick the 2-inch strip down.

4. Carefully center the picture.

5. Pull backing off while rubbing contact paper down.

2-inches

6. Then burnish it down or carefully iron it.

Step Two: Remove the paper.

After a good bond is obtained, remove the paper by soaking it in lukewarm water containing a wetting agent or mild detergent (these will speed up the removal of the paper). Five to 10 minutes after immersion, test by peeling off the backing material. Start at one corner and pull the paper away from the plastic. If the paper does not peel easily, reimmerse the visual. Thicker papers require a longer soaking time. If the water is too cool, the paper will peel off in small pieces. Once the backing paper is removed, avoid getting fingerprints on the visual by carefully handling it by the edges.

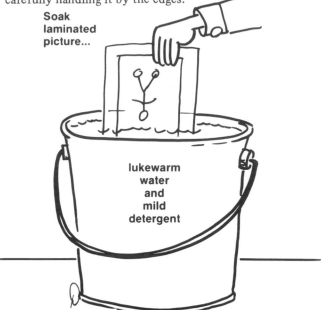

Soak laminated picture...

lukewarm water and mild detergent

Step Three: Remove the Clay.

A clay coating remains after the backing paper is removed. To remove this, lay the visual facedown on the table and wash it with a piece of cotton soaked in the soapy water. Carefully rub the entire surface at least four or five times, gently applying pressure from varying angles. Rubbing too vigorously may rub off the printer's ink.

Rinse in clear, cold water, handling the visual by the edges. Hang to dry in a dust-free area. Use clothes pins to hang on a line. Check the visual when dry to see that all clay particles have been removed. Any particles remaining appear as white and must be washed off; otherwise, they project as dark spots. A number of washings will not harm the transparency unless you rub too hard.

Carefully rub the sticky back with a piece of cotton that has been soaked.

Then rinse.

Step Four: Spray the visual.

The visual will be sticky on one side when all clay particles have been removed and the visual is dry. Spray this sticky side with a clear plastic spray to clear and preserve the transparency. Lay the visual on protective sheets of newspaper. Hold the spray can vertically about 10 inches from the transparency and spray, starting in the upper left-hand corner using a swinging motion from right to left and left to right. Uniformly spray the whole transparency, making sure to ventilate the spray area adequately. It is essential to spray evenly over the entire surface. Do not build up layers of spray the first time. Allow to dry. Spray again, if the transparency is streaked or sticky. Spray across the direction of the first coat.

Let dry...   Then spray with clear plastic.

Step Five: Mount the color lift.

Mounting will prevent color lifts from curling. Mount as you would any other transparency.

Mount it to keep it flat.

COLOR LIFTS USING A DRY-MOUNT PRESS

Color lifts may be made by using laminating film and a dry-mount press. Use the following procedure:

1. Set the dry-mount press at 270° for lamination material; 225° for Seal-Lamin.

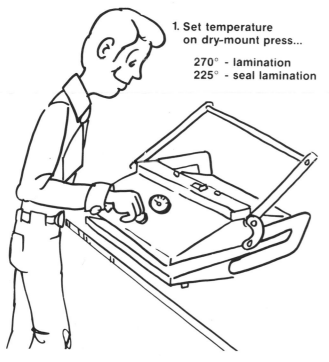

1. Set temperature on dry-mount press...

270° - lamination
225° - seal lamination

2. To drive out any moisture, dry the picture in the press for 45 to 60 seconds (if the humidity is high).

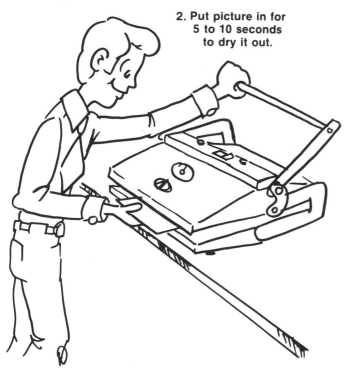

2. Put picture in for 5 to 10 seconds to dry it out.

3. Cut a piece of laminating film to cover the whole picture area. Make sure the surface of the picture is clean.

4. The dull side of the film has the adhesive and must be placed against the picture.

3. Cut lamination.

4. Remember the dull side is the adhesive side.

5. Trim off any excess lamination material that overhangs the picture more than ¼ inch.

5. Then trim to leave a 1/4-inch border.

1/4-inch

6. Smooth the film over the picture. To hold the film in place while putting it into the press, lightly tack the tip edges of all four corners.

7. Place an extra piece of heavy cardboard or masonite under the sponge rubber pad of the press to give extra pressure for laminating.

7. Place masonite or cardboard in press under the pad – to give extra pressure.

masonite

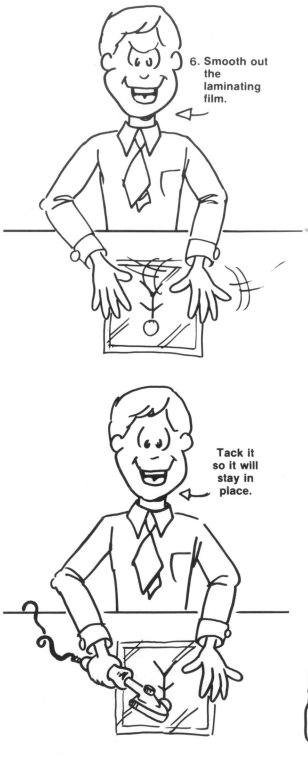

6. Smooth out the laminating film.

Tack it so it will stay in place.

8. Insert the picture between two protective sheets of newsprint, butcher, or release paper. This will protect the visual from dirt and residue of MT-5. Laminate for 45 to 60 seconds, depending on climactic conditions.

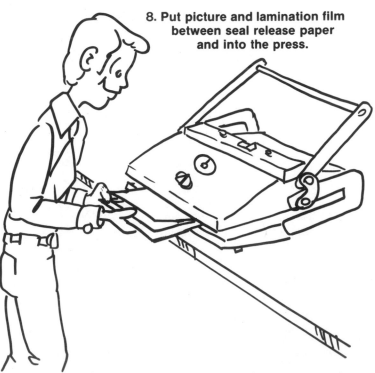

8. Put picture and lamination film between seal release paper and into the press.

**Pull down to close.
Leave in 45 to 60 seconds.
Lift up to open.**

LAMINATION MACHINE COLOR LIFTS

Any process capable of good plastic lamination may be used to make a color lift transparency. Generally, lamination machines bond the plastic to both sides of a page at once. Therefore, laminate two pictures back to back at one time. Thus, only the face of each picture will be laminated. Water may then soak off the backing paper. A thicker plastic coating may be obtained by running the pictures through the machine twice before separating and soaking. After the soaking process, run the material through the machine a third time. Lamination machines are capable of producing the best quality of color lift transparency.

9. Remove the picture from the press, and cool under a heavy weight for 2 to 3 minutes.

9. Immediately after removing picture from the press, place it under a heavy weight to cool.

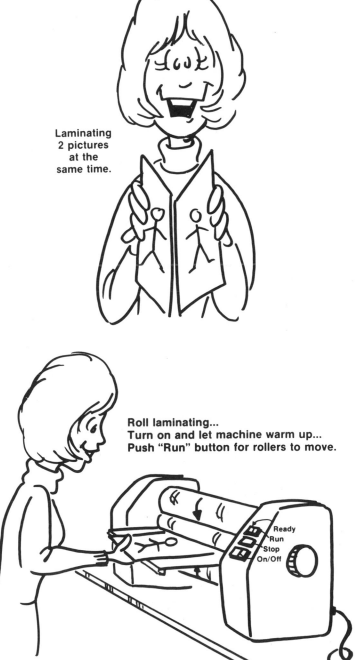

Laminating 2 pictures at the same time.

**Roll laminating...
Turn on and let machine warm up...
Push "Run" button for rollers to move.**

10. Bubbles and blemishes under the laminating film may be due to moisture. Reinsert the material into the press for an additional 45 seconds, and remove. After taking the color lift out of the press, immediately rub it vigorously with a cloth while it is still very hot. If bubbles persist, puncture them with a pin and reseal in the press again. Most often, vigorous rubbing will eliminate bubbles.

11. Soak off the backing paper following the steps outlined under steps 2 and 3, adhesive-backed plastic lamination.

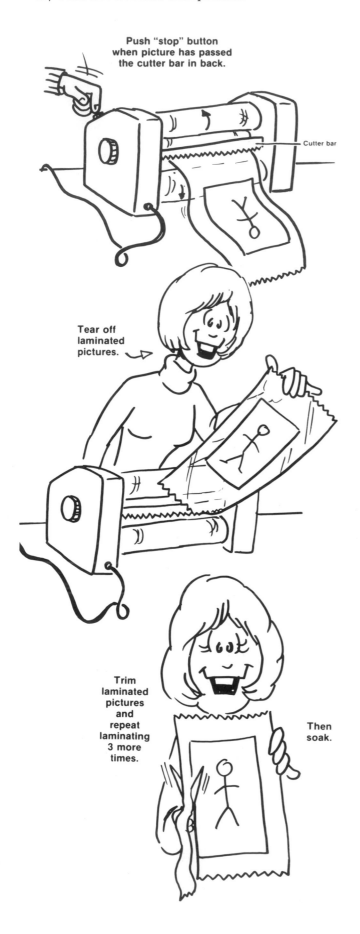

Push "stop" button when picture has passed the cutter bar in back.

Cutter bar

Tear off laminated pictures.

Trim laminated pictures and repeat laminating 3 more times.

Then soak.

TWENTY-FIVE IDEAS FOR USING COLOR LIFT TRANSPARENCIES

It is not recommended that color lift transparencies replace 35mm 2x2 slides. Slides are inexpensive and quick to produce. However, for a change of pace, or where photographic equipment is not available, low-cost color lift transparencies may be used. You may want to try some of these ideas:

1. Assign a task force of students to research a topic on a given country. Ask them to find pictures that illustrate their ideas. Make the pictures into color lift transparencies for purposes of reporting to the class. Save the transparencies for future use.

2. Assign students to find pictures that portray the feel or mood of a piece of music. Make the pictures into color lift transparencies. Project them as the piece is being played on a record or tape recorder. (An example: America the Beautiful).

3. Use color lift transparencies as part of a table display or interest center. Make a cube from heavy cardboard. Cut out windows, much like an overhead transparency mount. Mount the color lift transparencies similarly to overhead mounts. Tape the cardboard pieces to form a cube. Place a lamp inside the display to illuminate the transparencies.

4. Make reproductions of paintings into color lift transparencies. Use a water-soluble pen to diagram composition or to point out perspective.

5. Produce and project a color lift transparency of an animal, mountain scene, or flower. Ask students to write descriptions of what they see.

6. Use color lift transparencies to develop or drill vocabulary in English or a foreign language.

7. Use color lift transparencies to visualize dress, customs, and culture of people in other lands.

8. Use color lift transparencies to focus on the environment and environmental problems. Use as a focal point for discussion.

9. Use color lift transparencies to introduce a lesson or unit of study on a country or topic.

10. Use a set of color lift transparencies to take an imaginary field trip to a national park or city in the United States.

11. Use a set of color lift transparencies to present vocations. Use to stimulate discussion about jobs and trades.

12. Use color lifts of advertisements to discuss junk foods and proper diet.

13. Use color lifts to discuss interior decorating, color schemes, and styles of furniture.

14. Use color lifts to discuss current events and trends. Make maps, charts, and graphs into color lift transparencies for the class to study.

15. Mount portions of color lifts into small cardboard frames and shapes. Incorporate these into a mobile.

16. Black-and-white lifts are good masters for diazo transparencies. Many interesting effects can be produced. See chapter 8 for diazo transparency production.

17. Use color lift transparencies of magazine advertisements to stimulate discussion of truth in advertising and consumer protection.

18. Use color lift transparencies to illustrate elementary concepts in geography, such as rivers, lakes, peninsulas, and islands.

19. Use *Time* covers to present key business and political figures for social studies class or current events.

20. Try color lift slides for a change of pace. Insert a small piece of the color lift into a cardboard or plastic 2x2 slide mount. (You may buy these at camera stores.) Seal with a hot iron. (Ask for larger 127-roll film-size cardboard mounts.)

21. Use color lifts to compare types of housing around the world. Use as a springboard for discussion of the effect of climate on culture.

22. Use color lift transparencies to discuss the role of climate in the type of dress people wear. Make color lift transparencies of different types of dress around the world.

23. Use color lift transparencies to stimulate conversation in a foreign language. Use the transparencies as focal points for drills in ordering a meal in a restaurant, making conversation using vocabulary found in the picture, or using the language to describe what is in the picture.

24. Use old *National Geographics* to make a series of color lifts presenting the development of transportation in the United States.

25. Using old issues of *National Geographics*, contrast the dress and way of life in the United States today as compared with 25 or more years ago.

SUMMARY

Color lift transparencies are not as widely used as other types; however, they offer a change of pace. Color lift production may be used as a craft-type project for students. Students may use them to report ideas learned from research in the library/media center. Many writing, organizational, and communication skills may be learned through the production and utilization of color lift transparencies. Color lift is the only inexpensive way to produce four-color photographic overhead transparencies.

Thermographic (Heat) Transparencies

Low cost and speed of production make the thermographic process the most widely used in the public schools. Graphic material from newspapers, magazines, books, and brochures is used to produce transparencies in a matter of minutes. A number of companies market thermographic transparency materials. Here are three:

1. 3M Corporation
    Visual Products Division
    3M Center
    St. Paul, MN 55101

2. Columbia Ribbons and Carbon
    International
    Herbhill Road
    Glen Cove, NY 11542

3. Arkwright Incorporated (USI)
    Fiskeville, RI 02823

THERMOGRAPHIC PRINCIPLE

Basic to the thermographic process are dyes that activate at a certain temperature when passed by an infrared (heat) lamp. Carbon has the ability to absorb and store heat, thus activating the dye. Therefore, this may be called a carbon-heat process. Carbon-based materials must be used for master copy in the thermographic process. The most popular machine for producing thermographic transparencies is the Thermofax, Model 45, Secretary, copy machine. A belt transport system moves the master and transparency material past a heat or infrared lamp. Other machines on the market utilize types of rubber roller transport systems. Here is a list of materials that contain carbon and that may be used to produce transparencies:

Black printer's ink used to print newspapers, books, brochures, magazines, and mimeograph copy

India ink

Electrostatic copy (photocopying) is a powdered carbon process

#2 soft lead pencil

Reproducing typewriter ribbon

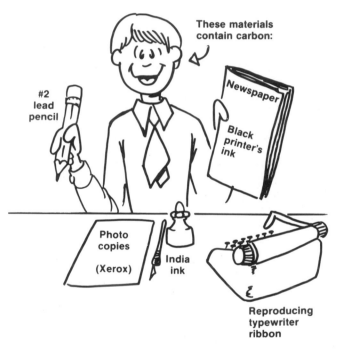

Certain, but not all, black felt or ballpoint pens will reproduce. Before using them, run a test to determine if they will reproduce. Some will reproduce but require much more heat than other marking devices. This creates the problem of how to set the copy machine dial correctly. Often, a correct exposure for a black felt pen is much too hot for a newspaper clipping. Therefore, printing captions for printed materials using a black felt pen or ballpoint creates a problem. Because various marking devices contain varying amounts of carbon, they are not all run at the same setting on the dial of the Thermofax machine. Pencil or pen lines require more heat than black, printed lines such as newspaper. A simple solution is to make a photocopy of the master, which will result in an even amount of carbon. Thus a caption added to a newspaper clipping using felt pen or pencil will contain the same amount of carbon as the clipping. Run the photocopy as the master. Material that will reproduce on the heat copy process is termed "faxable."

EXAMPLES OF FAXABLE MASTER MATERIALS

Hundreds of master artwork packets are marketed by the 3M Visual Products Division. A listing may be obtained by writing to: 3M Corporation, Visual Products Division, 3M Center, St. Paul, MN 55101. All types of printed materials may be used. Here is a list of readily available artwork:

Book illustrations	Coloring books
Newspaper cartoons	Outdated encyclopedias
Pen and ink drawings	Magazine advertising
Telephone yellow pages	Cartoon greeting cards
Children's storybooks	Mimeograph copy (black)
Catalogues	Calendars (for numbers)
Letterheads (logos)	Workbooks
Comic books	Handbills
Posters	Maps, charts, and graphs
Brochures and pamphlets	Restaurant place mats
Black rubber stamps	

CLIP ARTWORK

A number of companies market artwork for publication purposes. This artwork may be found in newspapers, advertising, fliers, and newsletters. It is also excellent for overhead transparencies. Clip art companies will send you a listing. Material is usually classified by subject.

Just cut and use.

Here are a few addresses:

American Mail Advertising	A. A. Archibold Publishers
61 Newbury Street	419 South Main Street
Boston, MA	Burbank, CA
Multi-Ad Services	Harry Volk, Art Studio
118 Walnut Street	Pleasantville, NJ
Peoria, IL	
Buckingham Graphics, Inc.	Gestetner Corp.
537 Custer Avenue	216 Lake Avenue
Evanston, IL 60202	Yonkers, NY 10702
Idea Art	Interstate Printers, Inc.
30 East 10th Street	19-29 North Jackson Street
New York, NY 10003	Danville, IL 61831

Product Aid Service Clips
Box 362
Westbury, Long Island, NY 11591

TYPES OF HEAT COPY MASTERS

The materials listed previously may be used as the basis for a number of different types of heat copy masters:

1. *Professionally published books of master artwork*, such as those marketed by 3M Visual Products Division.

2. *Tear sheets* that are pages torn out of workbooks, magazines, and books. The material is used mostly in its entirety. It may be used to explain a procedure or how to fill out a form.

3. *Traced masters* may be made by using a soft #2 lead pencil. This technique is used when pages may not be torn out of a book or a copy machine is not available.

4. *Electrostatic copy (photocopy)* is excellent heat copy master material because it is a carbon powder process. This material may be used to copy drawings in colored ink so that they are faxable.

5. *Typed masters* utilizing a reproducing ribbon on a primary or large type typewriter make acceptable masters. Do not use an elite or pica typewriter because the type is too small.

6. *Paste-up or assembled masters* material from a number of printed sources may be pasted or tacktaped to a layout sheet, and run as a master. Clip art, newspaper 'drawings, magazine artwork, and brochures are a few sources of printed materials. More instructions will be given on this process later in this chapter.

NOTE: You should be aware that utilizing some of these processes may be in violation of copyright laws. This subject is too involved to deal with here, but anything that eliminates a sale of copyrighted material is in violation of the copyright law.

TYPES OF THERMOGRAPHIC TRANSPARENCY MATERIALS

There are two main types of thermographic (heat) transparency materials marketed today: direct action dye, and activator sheet.

1. *Direct Action Dye.* This process uses heat stored by carbon to activate a dye coated to acetate. The dye is activated directly by heat. It should be noted that any heat, such as that from the sun, will activate the dye. Generally, the dye is black and is coated to clear, red, blue, yellow, or green sheets of acetate. The 3M Corporation is the largest marketer of these materials.

2. *Activator Sheet.* This process uses heat stored by carbon to release a chemical in an activator sheet to activate the dye. This process may use black, red, green, blue, or purple dyes. 3M, Columbia Carbons, and Arkwright Inc. (USI) market this material.

RUNNING DIRECT ACTION DYE MATERIALS

This material is designed to be run through a model 45 Thermofax Secretary copy or similar machine. This is a black line material that will have a notch in one corner. The notch is always placed in the upper right-hand corner, which indicates the dye is away from you or next to the master material. Because this is a direct-contact process, it is important for the dye to make good contact with the carbon-based material on the master.

1. Place transparency over the master as they come out of the machine.

Use these steps to run direct action dye materials:

1. Place the master so that the narrow end of the rectangle is up or toward the copy machine.

2. Place the acetate sheet over the master so that the notch is in the upper right-hand corner. The dye will then make direct contact with the master material (carbon). For better contact, place two to three sheets of typing paper under the master.

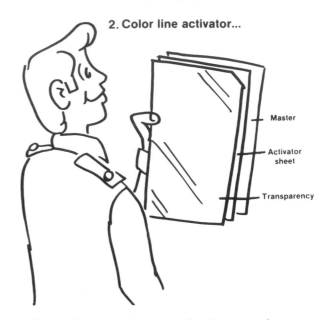

2. Color line activator...

3. Place the master between the lines on the entry way of the machine, and insert until the belt transport grasps the master. Release your grip and allow the machine to transport the master past the heat lamp.

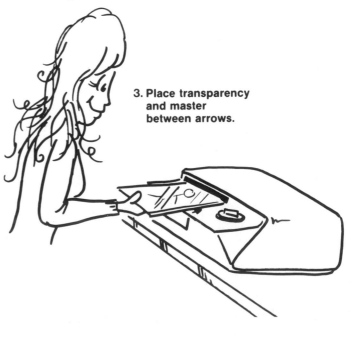

3. Place transparency and master between arrows.

4. Grasp the material as it comes out of the machine. Remove the transparency material, and project.

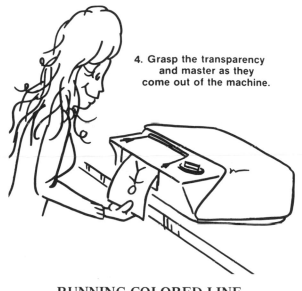

4. Grasp the transparency and master as they come out of the machine.

RUNNING COLORED LINE ACTIVATOR SHEET MATERIAL

Manufacturers package activator sheet materials differently. Generally, there will be a sheet of acetate, a packing sheet, and an activator sheet. The activator sheet will be shiny on one side; dull and rough on the other. The dull side contains particles of a white substance (chemical). Some companies place a notch in the upper right-hand corner. To run this material, follow these directions:

1. Place your master on a table surface. Remember, the rectangle should be placed so that the narrow width is placed into the machine.

2. Take the activator transparency material out of the box. If there is a packing sheet between the acetate and the activator sheet, discard it. Some materials may also have a carrier sheet beneath the activator sheet. Insert the master between the activator sheet and the carrier sheet (3M system).

3. Place the assembly over the master. The sequence should be: Master (on the bottom), activator sheet, acetate sheet (the transparency).

4. Run the material through the heat copy machine (Thermofax). Discard the activator sheet, and project the transparency. *NOTE*: The activator sheet may also be projected as a reversal transparency. You may want to experiment using activator sheets.

5. Remember, each sheet of acetate is coated with a single color dye. A separate sheet of transparency material and a master must be used for each color desired.

OBTAINING THE CORRECT MACHINE SETTING

There are several models of Thermofax Model 45 Secretary copy machines, along with a variety of rubber roller machines marketed by other companies. If the correct setting is not marked on the dial, it is wise to cut a sheet of transparency material into four strips, and run tests. The later Thermofax machines are speeded up by turning the dial clockwise and slowed down by turning it counterclockwise. If the lines on your test strip are weak and broken, turn the dial counterclockwise for more heat. If the letters bleed (are not crisp) or ghost images and specks appear, turn the dial clockwise for less heat. Mark the correct setting with a tab, a mark made with a felt pen, or a piece of masking tape. After a general setting has been determined, you will also find that different types of materials and marking devices require further adjustment of the dial. Generally, printer's ink, photocopies, and India ink require less heat than pencil lines. You should be aware that Thermofax Model 45 copy machines also run spirit masters, mimeograph stencils, pregummed mailing labels, and paper copies of letters.

RUNNING CLIPPED MATERIAL

Sometimes it is desirable to clip artwork from several sources and assemble a master. It is necessary before running this material to attach it to a sheet of paper so that it won't move before the image is affixed to the transparency material. This may be done by three ways:

1. Use an acetate or screen carrier. These may be purchased from the 3M Corporation.

1. Use an acetate or screen carrier like this for clip art.

2. Paste the clippings in place by using a small spot of rubber cement. Allow to set before running. Try to avoid hard particles of dried cement.

3. Tacktape into place with a thin acetate adhesive-backed tape. Tape only the leading edge that enters the machine first. Allow the trailing edge of the clipping to slip as it bends around the belt transport system of the machine.

NOTE: It is a good idea to make a layout sheet by tracing around a transparency mount with a nonreproducing pencil. You can then visualize how the mounted transparency composition will look so you won't paste material too close to the edge of the mount. See the chapter on design.

MAKING NONREPRODUCING LINES FAXABLE

Some drawings may contain parts printed in a colored line or may not have any outline at all. Weak lines or drawings printed in colored ink may be made faxable by going over the lines with a soft #2 lead pencil. India ink may also be used if the paper is of the quality that prevents lines from bleeding or getting fuzzy. Captions may be added to drawings by using a soft #2 lead pencil or India ink. Tracing outlines of a photograph may transform it into a live drawing which is then faxable.

DELETING MATERIAL

Unwanted detail, information, or captions may be deleted by using the following techniques:

1. Cut out any portion not to be produced using a razor blade or X-acto knife.

2. Block out areas to be deleted by covering them with typing paper.

3. If the deletion is only a temporary one, make an electrostatic (photocopy) copy of the original, cut out the unwanted part, and run the remainder as a master.

CORRECTING TYPEWRITTEN COPY

Sometimes a typing or spelling error is made when typing a master. It is not necessary to retype the complete master. Make corrections using these steps:

1. Type the corrected copy (a letter, word, or phrase) onto a sheet of typing paper.

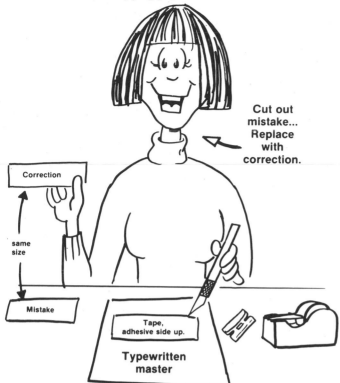

Cut out mistake... Replace with correction.

Correction

same size

Mistake

Tape, adhesive side up.

Typewritten master

2. Use a light table, or place the original against a window pane. Position the correction directly beneath the original (mistake). Align the letters so that they are in the same position as the original.

3. Use a razor blade or X-acto knife to cut out the mistake and the correction simultaneously. The cut usually will be a rectangle around the letter, word, or phrase.

4. Remove both cut-out pieces. Discard the error.

5. Place a piece of adhesive-backed acetate tape onto the back of the master. It should cover the cut-out area. The adhesive should be face up in the cut-out area.

6. Affix the cut-out correction in the cut-out shape, pressing it to the exposed adhesive of the tape.

7. Your correction is now complete. Run the master.

LINE OR PARAGRAPH CORRECTION OF TYPED MASTERS

If a larger portion of a master is to be corrected, cut out the unwanted section or error. Retype the section to be corrected. Assemble the material onto another layout sheet, using the same procedure for clipped material.

ADDING COLOR

Color may be added to heat copy transparencies in five ways:

1. Use a felt-tipped pen to color the desired area. Use techniques found in the chapter on handmade transparencies.

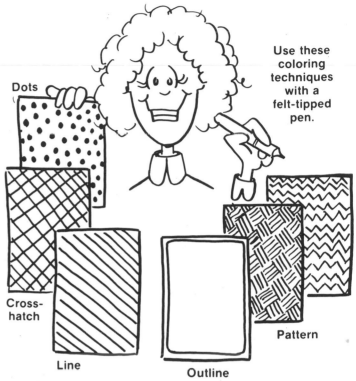

Use these coloring techniques with a felt-tipped pen.

Dots

Cross-hatch

Line

Outline

Pattern

2. Use colored line (activator sheet) transparency material. Place a master layout sheet over the original master. Use lines or shading with a soft #2 lead pencil to fill in the area to be in color. Use #2 pencil only for shading in smaller areas. Large areas may be colored by using a black felt pen or India ink to shade in the area to be in color. Remember, this must be done on a second master sheet. Large geometric shapes, such as circles, ovals, squares, or rectangles, may be cut from black construction paper. These shapes are affixed to a separate master sheet in the correct position, using double-edged tape or rubber cement. Next, run a photocopy (such as Xerox) of the felt pen or black construction paper shapes. This results in a carbon-coated area suitable for running as a heat copy master. On colored line activator sheet material, run rather slowly through the Thermofax machine. Sandwich-mount with the original transparency containing the

information. See Formats for Overhead Transparency Design in chapter 3. Mount as a base cell (sandwiched with original transparency).

3. Use colored acetate. Large, even areas of color may be obtained by sandwich-mounting strips or sheets of colored acetate with the base transparency. Geometric shapes may be cut out of a sheet of colored acetate so that a white area results. The viewer's eye is drawn to the white area. This is called billboarding. Generally, a black outline is used to cover the cutting line of the colored acetate. For additional information see Formats for Overhead Transparency Design in chapter 3 and the discussion of colored acetate in chapter 5.

4. Use colored adhesive material. Adhesive-backed color is marketed by 3M Corporation or may be purchased at graphic arts stores. It is the most professional-looking material for an even, solid area of color. Use the following steps when using colored adhesive material.

   Step 1. Place a white sheet of typing paper on the stage of the overhead projector. Use the stage as a light table.

   Step 2. Place the heat copy transparency over the white typing paper on the projector stage.

Step 3. Place a sheet of adhesive-backed colored material over the area to be colored. You should be able to see the transparency design through the adhesive-backed colored material.

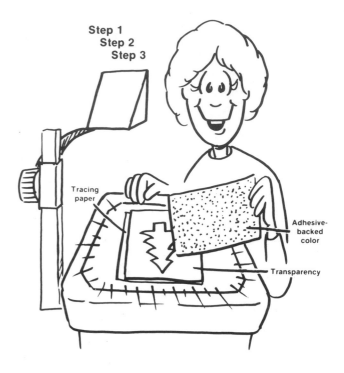

Step 4. Cut out a piece of the adhesive-backed color slightly larger than the area to be colored.

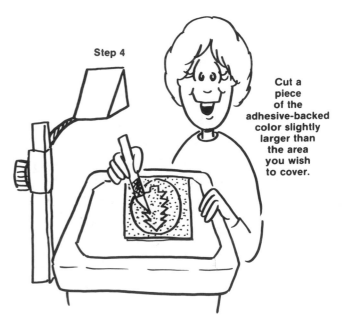

Step 5. Peel off the adhesive-backed color from the protective backing sheet, and affix it to the area to be colored.

Step 6. Use a razor blade or X-acto knife to cut around the outline of the area to be colored. Be careful to cut the adhesive-backed colored material and not the acetate.

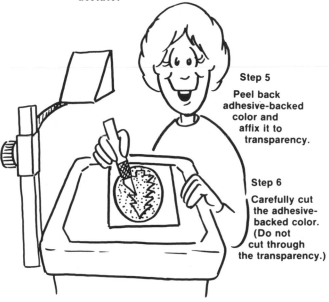

Step 5
Peel back
adhesive-backed
color and
affix it to
transparency.

Step 6
Carefully cut
the adhesive-
backed color.
(Do not
cut through
the transparency.)

Step 7. Peel off the residue and throw it away. Burnish the colored adhesive material, using a burnishing rod or blunt instrument. Don't be too concerned about tiny air bubbles as they generally won't show on the screen.

Step 7
Peel off
the extra.

Throw away
the scrap.

Burnish down
the adhesive-
backed color.

4. Use diazo film. See chapter 8 for procedures.

SIMULATING MOTION

A feeling of motion may be created by using a polarized spinner and polarized material. The direction that the spinner turns will determine the direction of motion on the transparency. Polarized material is marketed as adhesive-backed material. Cut to the proper size and shape and then affixed to the face of the transparency material. For a price quotation and further information, write to:

Technamation, Inc.
30 Sagamore Hill Drive
Port Washington, NY 11050

American Polorizers, Inc.
1500 Spring Garden Street
Philadelphia, PA 19101

American Animation, Inc.
6 East Spruce Street
Moorestown, NJ 08057

Polarized motion may be used to show electrical flow, blood circulation in the body, water flow, and other concepts requiring motion.

TRANSPARENCIES FROM ELECTROSTATIC COPY MACHINES

Almost any plain-bond copy machine will produce overhead transparencies on 3M brand PPC transparency film. Bond machines (manufactured by A. B. Dick, Apeco, Canon, Xerox, Toshiba, IBM, Kodak, and Saxon) are capable of producing transparencies. However, PPC transparency film will not work on roll-fed copy machines. When running transparencies, consider PPC film as you would paper. Set the exposure as you would for normal paper copies; then adjust light-dark settings from that point. Place one sheet of transparency film on top of the stack of paper, and run a test copy. If the transparency copy is good, try stacking and running multiple copies. Check your copy machine instructions for loading. The type and quality of the master will dictate the quality of overhead transparency. For further information, write to:

> 3M Corporation
> Visual Products Division
> 3M Center
> St. Paul, MI 55101

You may also want to check with the manufacturer of your copy machine to find out what overhead transparency materials are marketed by them.

SUMMARY

The thermographic (heat) copy transparency process requires carbon to activate the dye coated to the acetate sheet. Carbon absorbs and builds up heat from the lamp to activate various colored dyes. Black printer's ink, India ink, photocopy, #2 lead pencil, and reproducing typewriter ribbon are the materials most commonly used with the heat copy process. Material from newspapers, magazines, books, workbooks, newsletters, posters, and fliers may be quickly made into overhead transparencies to support local curriculum needs. The process is simple enough to be used by students in the classroom.

Diazo Transparencies

Although the cost of diazo is approximately the same as heat copy transparencies, the process is not widely used by classroom teachers. While the equipment for producing diazo transparencies is much less expensive than heat copy, it is more time-consuming to process. Diazo transparencies may be produced by using the following inexpensive materials: 1) a master; 2) a sheet of glass (to hold the master in close contact with the diazo film); 3) a source of ultraviolet light (such as a sun lamp); 4) diazo film; 5) a large gallon pickle jar (empty); 6) a piece of sponge (for the bottom of the pickle jar); and 7) a bottle of 28% ammonia (from a pharmacy). There are a number of commerically produced machines for exposing and developing diazo materials. Diazo film may also be exposed in a blueprint (white light) machine or by an offset printing platemaker.

The diazo process is directly associated with the chemistry of azo dyes. Diazo salts are affixed to the surface of the acetate. A single color is coated onto a sheet of acetate. Therefore, a separate master and sheet of diazo film must be used for each color desired. Exposure is not unlike photographic contact printing, except ultraviolet light is used. Wherever the ultraviolet light can strike the dye, it is burned off the acetate. Wherever the ultraviolet light cannot burn off the dye, it is developed by 28% ammonia fumes. Therefore, a diazo master must have opaque and translucent (or transparent) properties. Diazo film is marketed by two companies:

GAF Corp.
Photo and Repro Group
140 West Fifty-first
New York, NY 10020

Keuffel and Esser Co.
20 Whippany Road
Morristown, NJ 07960

Diazo film is marketed with colored or black line on clear background, or black line on colored background.

DIAZO MASTERS

A wide range of simple materials may be used to create diazo masters because the only requirement necessary is that the materials be capable of translucency and opacity.

Diazo masters:

You need these things to make diazo transparencies...

1. Tracing paper and India ink
2. Plastic
3. Blackline heat copy
4. X-ray film
5. Photographic negative
6. Photocopy machine

Here are but a few materials and methods for constructing diazo masters.

1. *Tracing paper*. Any high-quality paper permitting penetration by ultraviolet light, such as tracing or velum, is an excellent base material. Transparency images are produced by drawing opaque images with pencil, India ink, grease pencil, or by using opaque tapes. Check for watermarks in the paper as they may be opaque enough to print.

2. *Plastic*. Any clear or frosted acetate on which an opaque image is drawn produces an excellent diazo master. Here are some possibilities:

   A. *Frosted acetate*. The eched finish permits marking with soft lead pencil, crayon, India ink, ball point, dry transfer letters, or any opaque marking device.

   B. *Clear acetate*. To create a master, use opaque acetate ink (not India ink), black dry transfer letters, china marking pencils, or affixing opaque paper cut-out shapes.

3. *Black line heat copy*. Any black line, clear background, heat copy transparency serves as a good diazo master. 3M No. 533 black line material works well.

4. *X-ray film*. Diazo transparencies may be made by using X-ray film as a master or by clearing the film by immersing it in household bleach and marking on it with black acetate ink.

5. *Photographic negatives*. Black-and-white photographic films make professional-looking diazo transparencies.

   A. *Offset negatives*. Offset printing is a photographic process. Copy is photographed with a large bellows camera called a process camera. Therefore, any illustration can be photographed and the negative used as a diazo master. Remember, the image will be reversed, or a negative.

   B. *Enlarging method*. By using a photo enlarger, any roll film negative may be enlarged to the desired image size of 8x10 inches. The image is projected by the enlarger onto Kodalith Ortho Type 3 film instead of paper. The results are a photographic film positive rather than a paper enlargement. The film may then be used as an overhead black-and-white transparency or as a diazo master. The image may be changed to red, green, or blue by using diazo film. The film master is exposed the same as any other diazo master.

6. *Photocopying (electrostatic copy)*. Diazo is an excellent technique to make large, solid areas of pungent color. Color may be added to a heat copy or diazo black line transparency by using a photocopy machine. Make a copy of the master. Cut out areas where you do not desire color (so the ultraviolet rays can pass through and burn off the dye). Use as a master. A cut-out shape that is desired in color may be correctly positioned as a master by affixing it to a clear sheet of acetate with double-edged tape.

EXPOSING DIAZO MATERIAL

Each machine used to produce diazo transparencies will have an instruction manual. When using the sun lamp and pane of glass, use the following procedure:

1. Place a rigid piece of masonite or white cardboard at the base.

1. Make a master and sandwich assembly like this.

2. Next, place the diazo film with the emulsion side up. A notch in the upper right-hand corner will indicate that the emulsion is toward you.

2. Notch tells you what side has the emulsion on it.

3. Place the master over the diazo film so that the image side is down, next to the emulsion. For example, if the image has been drawn with India ink, place the ink next to the diazo film which has the emulsion side up.

4. Cover the entire assembly with a sheet of transparent glass. Make sure that the master and the film are in good contact everywhere.

5. Expose the sandwich to ultraviolet light. A sun lamp or the sun itself may be used to expose diazo film. You will have to run tests for correct exposure. To determine exposure, cut a sheet of diazo film into strips and run tests.

6. Remove the diazo film. You may not be able to see an image, but often a yellowish image is visible on the diazo film.

DEVELOPMENT PROCEDURE

The last step is the developing process. Follow this procedure:

1. Unscrew the lid of the gallon pickle jar. Make sure the jar is clean.

2. Place a small piece of sponge in the bottom of the jar.

3. Pour a small amount of the 28% ammonia on the sponge.

4. Insert the diazo sheet into the jar. Make sure the whole surface of the film is exposed to the ammonia fumes.

5. Tightly screw the lid to the pickle jar.

6. You can watch development take place through the sides of the pickle jar. Leave the diazo film in the jar until the color is the proper intensity. If removed too soon, the color may fade over time. (Be careful not to inhale the strong ammonia fumes, as they can be very irritating to the eyes, nose, and throat.)

7. Remove the transparency, and mount.

TRACED DIAZO MASTER

When making a traced diazo master, select material without a great deal of detail. Try to follow the guidelines set forth in chapter 3, "How to Design a Good Overhead Transparency." Scrub on as much carbon as possible so that lines are opaque. Weak lines will not reproduce well. A soft lead pencil allows you to erase mistakes. India ink may be used to make lines more opaque. Expose the master as presented in this chapter. Remember, it takes longer for ultraviolet light to penetrate tracing paper than clear plastics; therefore, exposure time will be much greater for traced masters than for masters using clear acetate base.

HEAT COPY MASTER

Clipped material from several sources may be pasted onto a heat copy master. Run a black line heat copy transparency, and use this as a diazo master. You may cut up the heat copy transparency, using each piece as a master to expose diazo material in several colors. If you wish an area of the transparency to be in solid color, use cut pieces of opaque paper to block the ultraviolet rays. Affix the opaque paper on the transparency master with double-edged tape. For example, if your transparency has four lines of type, by cutting out each line and exposing it to a different color of diazo film, each line may be projected as a different color.

MULTICOLOR DIAZO MASTER

Because of the vibrancy of color, diazo is excellent where color coding is necessary—for example, when it is desirable to visualize the system of veins and arteries in the human body, electrical circuitry, time lines, organizational charts, and maps. To produce a multicolored transparency, follow these steps:

1. Remember, each color desired on a transparency requires a separate master. Also, all masters should be in register (correct position) to form a whole. It is advisable to tape each master sheet into place; use paper clips or a clipboard so that masters maintain registration.

2. You should have some sort of master drawing from which to make a multicolored transparency. Tracing is perhaps the easiest way to make separate masters for each color. Mark four registration marks—one in each corner of the master drawing. Locate registration marks outside the picture area of the overhead frame. Registration marks may be dots or x's.

2. Determine the color you want.

Yellow

Blue

Black

3. Tacktape or fasten a sheet of tracing paper over the original visual. (You should have determined which portions of the drawing are to be in which color.) Trace registration marks at the four corners of the master.

4. Trace the base image (base cell). Usually, this would be printed as a black or dark color.

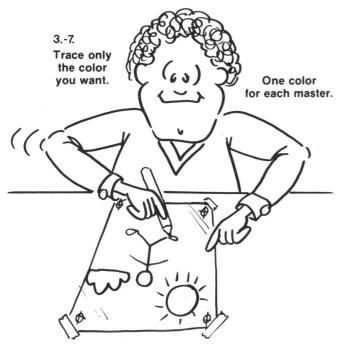

3.-7. Trace only the color you want.

One color for each master.

5. Remove the first tracing, and replace it with a second sheet of tracing paper. Trace the registration marks in each corner. Trace the portion that is to be in this color. Outside the picture area, write the color you wish this master to be.

6. Remove the second tracing, and affix a new sheet of tracing paper. Trace the registration marks. Trace the image to be in this color. Make a notation as to which color this transparency will be.

7. Repeat step 7 until all the desired colors have been drawn.

8. Take each master, one for each color, exposing it and developing it as presented in this chapter.

8. One master for each color.

Base Master

Blue Master

Yellow Master

9. A multicolor transparency may be mounted as a base cell or an overlay transparency. If it is to be a base cell, follow these steps:

A. Place the first or base transparency facedown on the back of the frame. This is usually the black line transparency. Tacktape only the corners to hold it in place.

A.-D. Tape corner.

Line up and tape.

Repeat for each color.

Tape all edges.

Base Cell

B. Add the next color transparency, using the registration marks in the corner to align it. Tacktape only the corners.

C. Add each color until all are tacktaped into place.

D. Tape all four sides of the transparencies to the frame. Use a good grade of masking tape.

If an overlay transparency is desired, follow these steps:

A. Place the black or base transparency on the back of the mount, facedown. Tacktape into place at the four corners.

B. Turn over (faceup). Carefully align the first color into place. If it does not fit properly, some adjustment may have to be made to the base cell (black transparency); if so, realign and tacktape. Tape one edge of the colored transparency to the face of the frame.

C. Position each colored overlay in turn, taping one edge of the acetate to the overhead frame. After the first overlay, you may use registration marks to help align each overlay.

D. Trim the edges of the acetate, if necessary, so that the overlays work easily.

E. Tape around all four sides of the base cell (black). Remember, the tape is the overlay hinge—it should work easily.

SUMMARY

The diazo process is gradually being replaced by an improved heat copy transparency process. It is not possible to obtain large areas of color approaching diazo quality with the heat copy process. However, graphic art departments still use diazo film when large, pungent, solid areas of color are needed. The diazo transparency is still the process to use to get the most professional-looking transparencies.

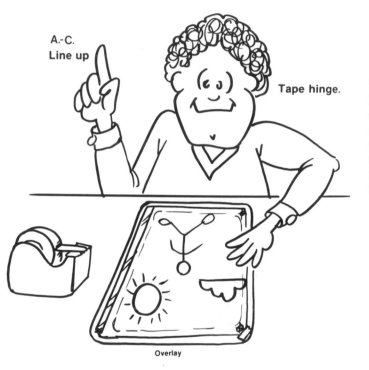

A.-C. Line up

Tape hinge.

Overlay

Mounting, Masking, and Overlays

Almost any hard cardboard, such as poster board, file folders, soap or cereal boxes, or other scrap cardboard, is suitable for making a transparency frame. Transparencies produced on 7 mil acetate (such as cleared X-ray film) may be used without mounting. The standard aperture (window) size for an overhead transparency frame is 7½x9½ inches. Aperture size may vary ¼ inch depending on the manufacturer. There are a number of advantages to mounting transparencies:

1. Mounting eliminates light leaks around the edges of a transparency, thus cutting down on glare.

2. Mounting assures that the transparency will lie flat.

3. Mounting permits easier handling by the presenter.

4. A presenter may make notes and write out questions to be asked on the edges of the frame.

5. Unmounted transparencies are very difficult to organize and file.

6. Mounted transparencies are easier to place into three-ring notebooks, transparency cases, and other storage facilities. They also may be numbered easily.

MOUNTING AN OVERHEAD TRANSPARENCY

A basic transparency is called a base cell (cel) and is mounted to the back side of a transparency frame. A base cell may be composed of a number of sheets of acetate, sandwiched and taped to the back of the frame. Information may then be added, or progressively revealed, by using mask and overlay systems. These are taped to the front or face of the overhead transparency frame. More information will be presented later in this chapter. The procedure for mounting a base cell (transparency) is as follows:

1. Select a clean, flat working surface, such as a table. Lay the transparency frame facedown onto the working surface.

Step 1
Mount a transparency.

2. Place the acetate sheet or sheets facedown onto the back of the frame (the image will appear backwards).

Step 2
Place transparency on mount.

Appears reversed

3. Manipulate the transparency until it is in the correct location. Tacktape into place with two or three small pieces of Magic Mending or masking tape.

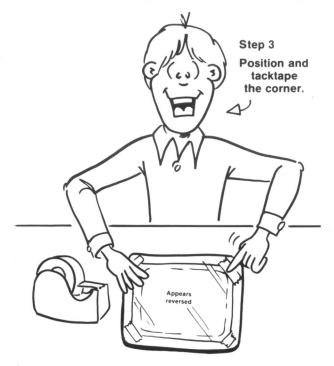

Step 3

Position and tacktape the corner.

Appears reversed

4. Flip the transparency over so that it is faceup. Check to see if the material is straight and not too close to the edge of the frame.

Step 4

Check it out.

5. Turn the transparency facedown again. Tape all four edges, using Magic Mending or masking tape. Failure to tape all edges securely may result in damage to the transparency when it is placed into a file or other storage facilities.

Step 5

Tape all edges.

NOTE: Because most screens are rectangular, a vertical transparency will bleed off the top and bottom of the screen. Therefore, vertical compositions should be used judiciously.

MASK SYSTEMS

Information on overhead transparencies may be progressively revealed by 1) marking, writing, or shading, 2) mask systems, or 3) overlays. The type of information placed on the transparency will usually determine the type of mask or overlay system to be used. Masks are cheaper to produce because only one sheet of acetate and scrap cardboard is used. A variety of notations may be written on the mask. Key ideas, questions to be asked, supplementary activities, and related materials written on a mask are helpful to the teacher.

Various types of scrap cardboard may be used to construct masking systems. The sides of soap boxes, cereal boxes, file folders, scraps of poster board, and cover stock (from print shops) are good materials for masks. Masking tape, Magic Mending, and mylar package tape are good hinge material. Remember, the tape is the hinge. Masks are attached to the front of the frame. Trim the tape at each end of the mask so that it will fold easily on the hinge.

TYPES OF MASKS

AREA MASK

There are two types of area masks, full and partial. A full area mask covers the whole aperture of the transparency mount. A partial mask may cover only a part of the transparency, allowing much of it to be projected onto the screen.

Area mask

To produce a full area mask, follow this procedure:

1. Mount the transparency before starting mask construction. The transparency must be designed so that it may be divided into two, four, six or more parts. When designing a mask-type transparency, you may want to leave space between objects to make it easier to mask off areas.

2. Cut a rectangular piece of cardboard so it covers the aperture (window) of the transparency frame, overlapping at least ½ inch on all sides. Thus, the mask should rest easily on all four edges of the frame. (Use a paper cutter so that cuts are straight and smooth.)

3. Use a paper cutter to cut the mask into two, four, or six parts, depending on the design. A piece of cardboard should cover each part of the drawing.

4. Assemble the pieces in place over the mounted transparency.

5. Tape the edge of the mask to the frame. Tape the edge that is to be folded. Remember, the tape is the hinge. Center the tape so that half the tape is affixed to the mask and half to the mount.

6. Trim the tape at both ends of the mask and between mask sections. The mask should fold easily and lie flat against the transparency frame.

7. Pull tabs may be made from folds of masking tape.

ACCORDION FOLD MASK

Steps 1 and 2 of the procedure for the accordion mask are the same as for the area mask. This mask is best used for progressively uncovering main points of a speech, lesson, unit of study, and what to look for in a film or field trip.

3. Cut the rectangular piece of cardboard into strips, each wide enough to cover the lettering of each point. Use the paper cutter to get straight cuts.

Design transparency.

Cut cardboard.

SPACE

BETWEEN

POINTS

1/2-inch larger than aperture

4. Place the strips in order on a smooth working surface. Leave a gap twice the thickness of the cardboard, or no less than 1/16th of an inch, between strips. Check to see that all gaps are equally spaced.

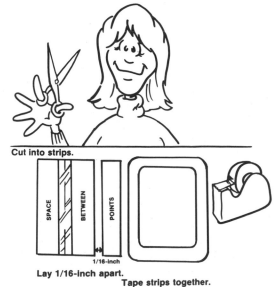

Cut into strips.

SPACE

BETWEEN

POINTS

1/16-inch

Lay 1/16-inch apart.

Tape strips together.

5. Tape each hinge at the gap, centering the tape over the gap. Use masking or mylar package tape. Each mask should fold freely and lie flat. If the masks are springy, probably not enough gap was left. Tape only the top side of the mask.

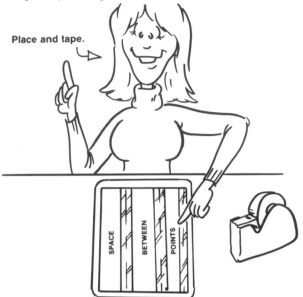

Place and tape.

6. Place the assembled mask in the correct position on the transparency frame. Tape the bottom edge of the mask to the frame. Center the tape, half on the mask and half on the frame. Trim the tape extending beyond each edge of the mask.

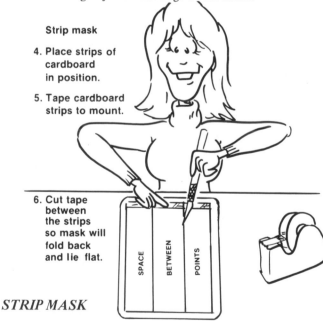

Strip mask

4. Place strips of cardboard in position.

5. Tape cardboard strips to mount.

6. Cut tape between the strips so mask will fold back and lie flat.

STRIP MASK

Strip masks are similar to the accordion fold except the strips are taped at one end rather than between masks. First, follow steps 1 through 3 of the area and accordion fold mask, then complete steps 4 through 6:

4. Place the assembled strips of cardboard on the transparency in correct order.

5. Tape the left or right edge of the masks. It is best to run one piece of tape down the full length of all the masks, half the tape on the mask, half on the mount.

6. Cut the tape at the top and bottom ends and between each mask. Cut only the half of the tape affixed to the mask. This will allow the mask to swing freely.

7. Swing the masks open so that they are lying flat to the left or right of the transparency. Run one strip of tape down the underneath side of the masks. Center the tape, one half on the mask, one half on the frame. Cut between the masks. This is the only mask system that is taped on the top and bottom. Because strip masks are long and narrow, there is very little area to tape for a hinge. Taping the top and underneath results in a stronger hinge and less sag.

The chief advantage of the strip mask over the accordion fold is its random access ability. It is particularly useful for teaching songs, poems, and quotations. Any section can be randomly revealed, whereas the accordion fold has a locked-in sequence.

PIVOT OR CIRCULAR MASK

This type of mask works well for foreign or English language drill. The circular mask has two windows opposite each other. A student turns the mask until two or more associated words or parts are revealed. The transparency has a circular design. The circular mask is held in place by a grommet, paper fastener, or thumbtack. The thumbtack is inserted from the bottom and is held on top by a small pencil eraser.

Look, it spins around.

SLIDING MASK

The sliding mask is very useful to progressively reveal main points of a speech, lesson, or unit of study. The mask is held to the overhead frame by a track constructed of strips of cardboard. Information is revealed by pulling the mask toward the bottom of the mount. Procedure:

1. Cut two strips of cardboard approximately ½ inch wide and slightly shorter than the length of the transparency frame. Use a paper cutter.

2. Staple these two strips along the opposite edges of the transparency frame. Take care to see that they are equal distances from top to bottom.

3. Cut the mask from a piece of cardboard, making it slightly narrower than the space between the two strips stapled to the transparency frame edge. The length of the mask should be sufficient to cover the desired area on the transparency.

4. Cut two strips of cardboard approximately ¾ inch wide, the same length as the ½-inch strips. Use a paper cutter to cut them so the edges will be straight.

5. Place the ¾-inch strips on top of the ½-inch ones, aligning them so that there is a ¼-inch overhang on the inside toward the mask. This overhang forms the track so the cardboard mask will not fall off the transparency.

6. Staple the ¾-inch strips to the ½-inch strips in at least three or four places.

Step 5
3/4-inch strip goes on top of 1/2-inch strip. Like so.

Step 6
Staple 3/4-inch strip to 1/2-inch strip.

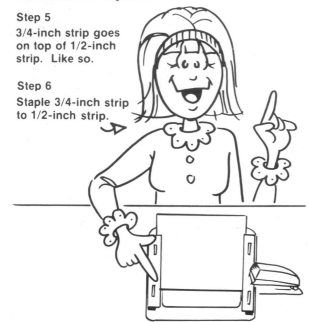

7. Insert the mask that you have cut (following instructions in step 3). The mask should move freely on the tracks. If it binds, check to see that there is enough of a gap between the mask and the two tracks. A pull tab may be made by using a folded piece of masking tape.

Step 7
Make sure it slides freely...

Tape pull tab

COMBINATION MASK

The arrangement of material on a transparency may lend itself to a number of different mask configurations. For example, a list of words may be revealed using a strip/ accordion fold mask. Each strip would cover a column of words. Any mask that is easily manipulated can be used to reveal information progressively.

CONTROLLED READER MASK

Use a long sheet of paper, cut to width so that it covers the complete aperture of the mount. Cut a long slit in the mask, uncovering a single line of type. Manipulate the mask by pulling it down to reveal quickly one line of type at a time. A tachistoscopic effect may be obtained by flashing the image briefly onto the screen. This mask may be used to develop reading skills or to aid with recognition of words or symbols.

FLIP-FLOP MASK

The flip-flop mask covers one-half of the transparency aperture and may be pivoted to cover either half. Use the following steps:

1. Divide the transparency aperture (window) into two equal parts. Make a light pencil mark at the center point on the transparency frame.

2. Use a paper cutter to cut a piece of cardboard that will cover one-half of the aperture of the frame, extending one-quarter to one-half inch beyond the edge of the aperture.

3. Place the cardboard so that it covers one-half of the aperture. Line up with the pencil mark at the center point on the frame.

4. Run a single piece of mylar or masking tape the full length of the mask at the center point. The tape should be centered, half on the mask, half on the acetate.

5. Trim the tape at both the top and bottom edges of the mask. The tape is the hinge and the mask should pivot on the tape hinge.

6. Pivot the mask over to lay on the second half of the transparency. Run a second piece of tape, centered half on the mask and half on the acetate. Trim at the top and bottom.

Your flip-flop mask should pivot easily to cover either half of the transparency. Use this for a short quiz: one-half for the questions and the other for the answers.

OVERLAYS

Masking does not lend itself to all types of transparencies. In some cases, the composition of the transparency cannot be divided into parts. Wholistic type transparencies require information to be added by the use of overlays. Here are some examples:

1. *A map.* When presenting trade routes, road systems, or names of geographic locations, mask systems are difficult to use.

2. *Internal workings of machines.* Overlays can present component parts of a machine and how it operates.

3. *Visually compare two objects, shapes, or areas.* The relative size of two countries may be quickly visualized by using a base cell for one country and an overlay for the other.

4. *Labeling a drawing.* Overlays are helpful when vocabulary or labels are added to a drawing (for example, the drawing of a human heart to which the names of each part are added).

TWO TYPES OF OVERLAY SYSTEMS

There are two types of overlay systems, fixed and random sequence.

1. *Fixed Sequence.* When information to be presented does not vary in sequence, all overlay sheets are mounted to the same edge of the mount. For example, the sequence is fixed when the exploration route of Magellan is progressively presented.

2. *Random Sequence.* Each overlay must be mounted to a different edge of the frame if a random sequence is desired. For example, when presenting the vegetable produces, mineral resources, industrial development, and rainfall of a given country, a random access overlay system is best.

RANDOM SEQUENCE OVERLAY SYSTEM

This is one type of overlay system

FIXED SEQUENCE OVERLAY

OVERLAY

ATTACHING OVERLAYS

Although there is no single best method to attach overlays to a transparency, here are two of the most popular techniques:

STAPLED FOLDED TAPE METHOD

Procedure:

1. Cut off a piece of Magic Mending or mylar package tape approximately 2 inches long. *NOTE*: Do not use inexpensive adhesive-backed acetate tapes. The adhesive life is approximately three years and will

not hold beyond that time. Mylar package tape is a tough, brown tape which may be purchased at office supply stores.

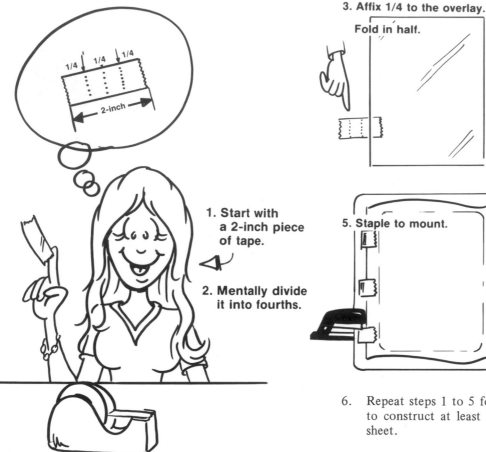

1. **Start with a 2-inch piece of tape.**

2. **Mentally divide it into fourths.**

2. Mentally divide the 2-inch piece of hinge tape into fourths (½-inch sections). Affix one fourth (½ inch) of the tape (adhesive side up) on the underside of the overlay sheet.

3. Fold the tape in the center (1 inch). Affix the last quarter (½ inch) to the top of the overlay sheet, above the first quarter already attached to the underside.

4. Two quarters (1 inch folded) should now be stuck together extending ½ inch beyond the overlay sheet. Two quarters should be affixed to the overlay sheet, one quarter on each side of the overlay sheet.

5. Staple the two quarters (½ inch) protruding beyond the acetate overlay to the transparency frame.

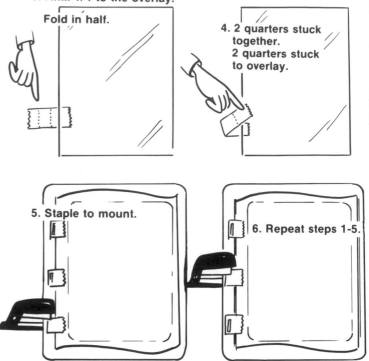

6. Repeat steps 1 to 5 for each overlay. It is advisable to construct at least three hinges for each overlay sheet.

7. If the overlays have a fixed sequence, staple all overlays at the same point to one side of the transparency frame.

8. If a random sequence for the overlays is desired, staple the hinges of each overlay to a different side of the transparency frame. *NOTE*: Hinges may be made from mylar packing tape (brown), furnace-duct tape (silver), Magic Mending tape (clear), book-mending tape (various colors), or Mystik tape (various colors). These materials are available at discount or office supply stores.

TAPING WITHOUT STAPLES

Procedure:

1. Tape the base cell to the back of the transparency frame. See "Mounting an Overhead Transparency" in the beginning of this chapter.

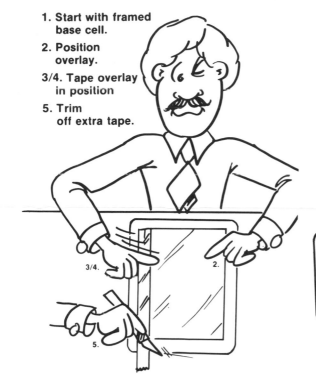

1. Start with framed base cell.
2. Position overlay.
3/4. Tape overlay in position
5. Trim off extra tape.

2. Position the overlay on the front of the transparency frame so that it is in register with the base cell (in proper position).

3. Use (or cut) tape to a ¾ inch width. Magic Mending tape, mylar packing tape, or masking tape may be used. Pull out a piece of tape long enough to cover the length of the overlay.

4. Affix the tape to the overlay and transparency frame so that half the tape is on the acetate sheet and half is affixed to the frame.

5. The tape may be trimmed to the exact length of, or may be extended beyond, the ends of the overlay sheet. If the tape extends beyond the end of the overlay, cut the tape affixed to the overlay so that it allows the overlay to be folded back easily. Remember, the tape is the hinge.

6. Sometimes it is necessary to trim the overlay sheets so that they may be manipulated easily. If the overlay is too wide to lie flat when laid over the base cell (butts up against the hinge of the opposing overlay), trim until it fits.

CUSTOM-MADE FRAMES

Generally, the standard aperture (window) of an overhead transparency frame is a rectangle 7½x9½ inches. However, various geometric-shaped apertures may be used, such as:

1. An oval

2. A circle or number of circles

3. A combination of circles and rectangles

4. Abstract geometric shapes

5. Rectangular slits

6. A combination of large and small squares or rectangles

Do-it-yourself custom frame.

USING TRANSPARENCY FILM

Color film, such as Ektachrome, is available in 120 roll film size for use in single or dual lens reflex cameras. The 120 film size when developed is 2¼x2¼ inches. These larger format transparencies may be mounted onto a transparency frame along with other transparency material. Two apertures (windows) must be cut in a frame, one for the 120 transparency and one for heat copy material. Here are some examples of the use of this technique:

1. A picture of a student who has written the poem, song, or idea presented on the transparency.

2. A picture of the composer or writer of the music or literature being presented.

3. A photograph of a musical instrument being featured while the sheet music is projected. Both may be presented as the piece of music is being played on a tape recorder or record.

4. A photograph of an explorer while a map of his exploration route is being presented.

Both the photograph and the larger transparency material may be manipulated during a presentation.

STRIP FILM MOUNT

Blends, prefixes, suffixes, and tenses in language may be presented, using a manipulative strip of acetate. The acetate strip is held to the transparency mount by slits cut in the cardboard. Here is the procedure for making a strip film mount:

1. Cut a piece of cardboard the usual size for an overhead mount (10x12 inches).

2. Cut a narrow rectangular aperture in the center of the overhead mount.

3. Cut four slits slightly longer than the width of the aperture—two above and two below the rectangular aperture.

4. Write the root word on acetate in the correct position, and place on the back of the mount over the rectangular aperture.

5. Cut the acetate strip or strips to the desired length. Write the prefixes, blends, etc. on the acetate strip.

6. Insert the acetate strip into the slits above and below the rectangular aperture. Manipulate by pulling upward or downward to expose the prefix or blend.

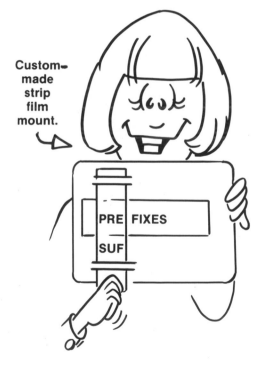

Custom-made strip film mount.

PRE FIXES

SUF

MANIPULATIVE FIGURES

Flannelgraph figures or other drawings may be traced onto heavy 7 mil acetate strips or pieces. These figures may be manipulated over a base cell depicting a background scene. For example, the story of Little Red Riding Hood may be visualized by using heavy acetate figures of the wolf, grandmother, the bed, and Little Red Riding Hood. Manipulate the figures over the background scenes. Remember, the overhead is the "flannelgraph" of the projected world.

DIALOGUE MOUNT

Make a heat copy transparency of two figures engaged in a dialogue. Place these at the bottom of the transparency. At the top, draw two dialogue balloons like those used in comic strips. Use a water-soluble pen to write dialogue in English or foreign languages. You may set up the dialogue of one character and ask a student to come write the response. Overlays may be used to change the facial expressions of the two characters.

FILE FOLDER MOUNT

Tagboard file folders are excellent for making overhead transparency frames. Cut any size of aperture from one side of the folder. Mount a transparency on the inside of the folder. To project, open the folder and place it on the projector stage. Notes or questions may be written on the other side of the folder. File in a steel, cardboard, or other file cabinet. A variation is to cut two apertures, one on each side of the folder. Mount a base cell on one side and an overlay on the other. Fold or close the folder to add the information on the overlay.

NOTES

FILE FOLDER FRAME

MATERIALS FOR CARDBOARD OVERHEAD MOUNTS

Any scrap of cardboard 10x12 inches may be used to produce an overhead transparency frame. Here are a few materials:

The sides from a large soap box

The sides from a large cereal box

Protective sheets between X-ray film

Manila envelopes

Tagboard or cover stock from a print shop

Poster board (or old signs)

CARDBOARD STRIP FRAME

Cut eight strips of cardboard approximately 2½ inches wide. Make four of the strips 10 inches and four 12 inches long. Place two strips on each end (10 inches) and two strips on each side (12 inches). Place the strips so that they overlap the transparency acetate by ½ inch. Staple into position, placing several staples through the acetate and cardboard, and several along the outer edges of the cardboard. The overlapping thickness of the cardboard at the four corners gives added strength and protection to the mount.

L-SHAPED STAPLED FRAME

This is a variation of the stapled strip frame. Cut four pieces of cardboard in the shape of an L, 10x12 inches. Make the L 2½ inches wide. Position the L's so that they form a frame surrounding the transparency. Place two L's on top of the acetate and two below. Staple into place. *NOTE*: Holes may be punched into frames with a three-holed paper punch. This permits the storing of transparencies in a three-ring notebook.

INSTAFRAME

Instaframe is a thermoformed plastic frame held securely to the projector stage by four rubber skidproof pads. An 8½x11¼ frame will allow unmounted multiple sheets of transparency material to be placed on the projector. This eliminates mounting or the taping of overlays. This also permits the filing of transparencies in pocket or file folders. For further information, write to:

Faith Venture Visuals, Inc.
P. O. Box 685
Lititz, PA 17543

ACETATE ROLLS

The acetate roll attachment is available for most projector models at a local audiovisual dealer. Material prepared ahead of time is rolled onto the projector stage at the moment needed. These rolls are useful to present material too long or large to be presented on mounted transparencies (such as a time line or a genealogy).

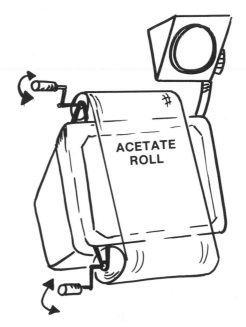

SUMMARY

Mounting transparencies to rigid cardboard frames protects them from damage, eliminates glare when projected, and facilitates storage and retrieval. Transparencies are mounted to the back of the frame and are called base cells even though a sandwich of several sheets of acetate is used. Information may be progressively revealed on the overhead by writing with a pen, then uncovering a mask or laying over an additional sheet of acetate. Mask systems are low cost because they are made from scrap cardboard. Some common mask systems are area, accordion fold, strip, sliding, pivot and flip-flop. When transparencies cannot be divided into component parts, such as with mask systems, additional information may be revealed by using overlays. These are useful in labeling parts of a drawing (such as the human heart), maps, and charts. Overlays may be taped to one edge of the frame, giving a fixed sequence of material, or one overlay to each edge of the frame for a random sequence of information. Creative manipulation of masks and overlays can add interest and excitement to a lesson.

Organizing Overhead Transparencies for Teaching

Although one of the main advantages of the overhead transparency is its compactness and ease of storage, some type of storage and retrieval system is needed. Such a system should be organized so that a teacher may retrieve the right transparency at the right time. A teacher may have hundreds of transparencies at his or her fingertips by utilizing a storage system. Perhaps no other medium has greater accessibility.

UNMOUNTED TRANSPARENCY STORAGE

If transparencies are produced on heavy acetate, such as cleared X-ray film, they need not be mounted. However, odd-sized pieces of acetate should be avoided because they are awkward to store and retrieve. It is best to standardize transparencies on 8x10-inch sheets. Here are some storage ideas:

File Folders. File folders are an inexpensive way to organize and store transparencies according to topics. Usually, the folders must themselves be stored in a larger container, such as a steel file cabinet or cardboard box.

Pocket Folders. Pocket folders may be made from tagboard or purchased at office supply stores. Transparencies held in place by a pocket are not as apt to slip out and be lost as is the case with file folders. File folders may be made into pocket folders by stapling or glueing in a pocket. Print shops sometimes have leftover tag or cover stock that is ideal for making pocket folders.

Clasp Folders. Clasp folders will securely hold transparencies that have been punched with a three-hole paper punch. These folders are available at office supply stores. Pocket and clasp-type folders may be organized and stored in a pam box, art folder, or cardboard box.

Three-ring Notebooks. Garage sales, the Goodwill, and Salvation Army stores often have inexpensive, secondhand three-ring notebooks. Punch three holes into the acetate with a paper punch, and insert into the notebook. Each notebook may be organized around a topic, unit of study, or lesson. Notebooks may be labeled and stored on a bookshelf.

Check out these storage ideas...

Pocket folder

File folder

Clasp-type folder

Look at these inexpensive ways to store transparencies...

cardboard box

3-ring notebook

Cardboard Boxes. Hosiery, heat copy transparency, and other boxes 8½x11 inches are excellent for storing unmounted transparencies. Label each box and store in a pam box or steel file drawer.

MOUNTED TRANSPARENCY STORAGE

Generally, it is wise to mount heat copy transparencies. Mounting protects them, and gives rigidity for filing, storing, and retrieving. Here are some ways to store transparencies for easy retrieval.

File Cabinets. Metal filing cabinets will store hundreds of transparencies. Transparencies are grouped by subject or in a sequence of lessons. Heavy cardboard separator sheets are used to divide them into some type of classification system.

These file cabinets are great for storage...

Cardboard Files. Inexpensive, legal-size cardboard file cabinets are sold at office supply stores and discount houses. The purchaser usually must assemble the cabinet.

Apple Boxes. One of the least expensive storage containers is the apple box. Apple boxes are often given away by the produce department at the local supermarket. It is best to cut them down to facilitate storage and retrieval of folders and transparencies. Cut the box at a slant from the back to the front. Leave a height of about 11 inches in the front. You may want to cover the box with adhesive-backed vinyl (contact) to make it

more attractive. Use heavy cardboard separator sheets to organize units of study or topics. When the lid is used to cover the file, the boxes may be stacked one on top of the other so that hundreds of transparencies are stored in a small space.

You can create your own. Cut on dotted line.

Apple box

Pamphlet Boxes. Pam boxes have long been used by librarians to store odd-shaped pieces of printed material. They are excellent for storing transparencies. You can make your own pam box from a large, family-size soap box. Cut the top off so that you can reach into the box and retrieve the transparency. Decorate the box with adhesive-backed shelf vinyl or by gluing surplus gift wrapping paper to the box with rubber cement. The best procedure is to use rubber cement to coat the back of the gift wrapping and all four sides of the box. Allow the cement to dry completely (until dull). Next, affix the gift wrapping paper to the outside of the box. Attractive magazine pictures or wall paper may be used instead of gift wrapping paper.

These pamphlet boxes you can make yourself.

Three-ring Notebooks. Punch three holes into the transparency mount, and store transparencies in three-ring notebooks. Label the spine of the notebook, and store on a bookshelf.

Manila Envelopes. Large manila envelopes may be cut on one or two sides to facilitate inserting transparencies for storage. Organize envelopes into lessons or topics. Envelopes then are stored in file cabinets or other storage containers.

Art Folders. Accordion-type art folders are good storage containers for instructors who are moving from place to place. These folders are usually secured by a tie string.

Plastic or Steel File Boxes. Office and school supply stores sell plastic file boxes made especially for overhead transparency storage. However, any personal record file box large enough to store a transparency may be used. File boxes are particularly useful to store transparencies for a unit of study. They are very compact and durable.

Plastic Dishpans. If students are to have access to transparencies, a dishpan full of them may be placed on a table or desk. This is particularly helpful when using transparencies for a unit of study.

Wire Record Rack. Transparencies may be at the teacher's fingertips by placing them on his or her desk in a wire record rack. Use this idea for transparencies that you may refer to daily for a period of time, such as math theorems.

Plywood Bin. A plywood bin in a classroom or library permits students and teacher access to hundreds of transparencies. Many of these transparencies may be student-produced. Masonite or cardboard separators may be used to organize the transparencies into topics or units of study. Screw-on coffee table legs hold up the bin to a correct height for students.

Tote Box. A tote box just the right size for storing overhead transparencies may be cut from a cardboard box. Use a dowel or ruler inserted in both ends for a handle. Decorate the tote box with adhesive-backed vinyl shelf covering, or use rubber cement to affix gift wrapping paper, wall paper, or pictures. See pam box.

Tote boxes are useful to carry materials into the classroom for an overhead transparency workshop or in the classroom when students are producing transparencies. Acetate sheets, pens, frames, and tape stored in a tote box give students quick access to materials.

SUMMARY

Low-cost local production enables a teacher to have hundreds of transparencies to support local curriculum needs. Optimum utilization requires a storage and retrieval system so that the right transparency may be located and used at the right time. Storage and retrieval systems may also be designed for student access. Pocket clasp and file folders may store transparencies for individual lessons and, in turn, are stored in pam boxes, steel or cardboard file cabinets, or apple-box files. Transparencies placed in wire record racks, plastic dishpans, tote boxes, or bins are easily accessible to students. Only if a teacher develops a storage and retrieval system can the overhead be utilized to its fullest.

Ideas for Utilizing the Overhead Projector

Large image size and manipulation capabilities make the overhead the most versatile of all projectors. Also, the ability to use real objects, cut-out paper shapes, images drawn onto clear plastic, mask systems, and overlays results in the overhead being used in thousands of ways. Who is to say how an overhead may or may not be used? For more than 10 years, the author collected ideas for utilizing the overhead only to come to the realization that there is no end to possibilities. When 501 ideas were reached, the author simply said, "enough." But, there are probably this many and more ideas being used by teachers. It is hoped that you will try some of these ideas and will adapt them to your curriculum needs. In some cases, several ideas may be combined or used together. Don't hesitate to experiment and to test your own ideas on using the overhead. That is how these ideas were born.

ART EDUCATION

1. *Formal and informal balance.* Manipulate pieces of cut paper to demonstrate the basic principles of formal and informal balance. Demonstrate symmetrical and asymmetrical balance.

2. *Lettering styles.* Clip lettering from graphic arts catalogues, such as Chartpak, and make a heat copy transparency visualizing the basic differences in lettering style (such as Roman, Gothic, and text).

3. *Type size.* Use lettering clipped from a graphic arts catalogue to demonstrate how type is measured in points, such as 6, 24, 48, or 120 points.

4. *Rhythm and movement.* Visualize rhythm and movement in a composition by using a felt pen to draw repetitive patterns of lines on a clear acetate sheet.

5. *Still life arrangement.* On a separate piece of heavy acetate, draw each of the objects used in a still life. Use this material to demonstrate possible arrangements of a still life.

6. *Primary and secondary colors.* Use pieces of colored acetate to visualize primary and secondary colors by overlapping red, blue, and yellow.

7. *Mixing colors.* Use food coloring and water in a petri dish to visualize how the mixing of primary colors forms secondary colors.

8. *Warm and cold colors.* Use colored acetate sheets to demonstrate warm and cold colors. Project colored light onto a still life to study how the light source changes the colors in a still life.

9. *Perspective.* Use overlays to visualize the concept of one-point and two-point perspective.

10. *Proportion.* Use a base cell and overlays to visualize the proportions of parts of the human body.

11. *Facial structure.* Make a color lift transparency of a face. Use a water-soluble pen or overlays to point out facial structure.

12. *Logos.* For graphic arts, visually compare various logos taken from printed sources.

13. *Spotlight.* Use the overhead as a spotlight for a figure or still life drawing.

14. *Ceramic tools.* Use a transparency of basic ceramic tools when discussing their functions.

15. *Ceramic techniques.* Use line drawings to visualize ceramic techniques, such as coil, slab, slab-coil, and mould methods.

16. *Pottery*. Use the overhead to visualize the five states of ceramic pottery.

17. *Mobiles*. Use drawings of various mobiles to present the concept of mobile suspension as developed by Alexander Calder.

18. *Composition*. Project a transparency of a painting or drawing onto butcher paper taped to the wall. Use felt pens to analyze the composition.

19. *Art enlarger*. Use the overhead as an art enlarger for creating large paintings, murals, and stage scenery.

20. *Instructions*. Place step-by-step instructions for a project on a transparency, and project it so that students can refer to it while they work.

21. *Potato or block prints*. Have students print a sample of a potato or block print onto acetate. Use samples to show new students possible design ideas.

22. *Lettering*. Clip lettering from newspapers, magazines, brochures, and the like. Make the letters into a transparency, and project them onto posters or banners for use as lettering guides.

23. *Light table*. Use the overhead as a light table by covering the stage with white typing paper.

24. *Graphic design*. Make transparencies of business cards, letterheads, trademarks, and advertisements to visualize various graphic arts techniques in the use of type or design. You may have to make a photo copy to use as a heat copy master.

25. *Shading techniques*. Draw with a permanent pen, the objects of a still life. Use a water-soluble pen to demonstrate shading techniques of lines, cross-hatching, and dots. Demonstrate how shading will change as the direction of the source of light changes.

26. *Emotion of color*. Run a heat copy transparency of an illustration or drawing. Use different colored sheets of acetate to lay over the drawing. Use to discuss different types of feelings that color evokes.

27. *Silhouette drawings*. Use the overhead as a light source. Stand students in front of the lens so that their profiles are projected onto a wall. Tack up butcher paper, and trace the profiles with a pencil or felt pen.

28. *Shapes*. Place geometric forms cut from paper and real objects (such as scissors) onto the projector stage. Enlarge onto colored paper tacked to the wall. Trace with a pencil or felt pen. Cut out shapes and use to make large collages, murals, or for room decoration. Project onto cardboard to create materials for a mobile.

DRAMA

29. *Stage directions*. Use a transparency to demonstrate stage directions.

30. *Parts of a stage*. Visualize the parts of a stage, such as the proscenium, wings, and the like.

31. *Stage lighting*. Use a base cell of the floorplan and overlays to show acting circles and how acting areas are lighted.

32. *Greek theater*. Use a series of transparencies to visualize the development of Greek theater.

33. *Character movement*. Make a base cell of the floorplan. Use cut-out shapes representing each character. Manipulate the cut-out shapes to demonstrate character movement in a scene.

34. *Make-up*. Use a transparency of a face. Use a water-soluble felt pen to visualize make-up application.

35. *Flat construction*. Use a series of transparencies to visualize the construction of a standard flat.

36. *Bracing of stage scenery*. Use a series of transparencies to visualize the placement of rigging and bracing hardware.

37. *Background scenery*. Use transparencies for background scenery for role playing and drama. Rent or make a rear projection screen. Use a frosted plastic shower curtain, tacked to a 2x4 frame, for a rear screen. Place the projector behind the screen and the players in front. Change transparencies for scene changes.

38. *Cut-out puppets*. Draw a background scene onto plastic. Make cut-out paper puppets (which will project as a shadow or black). Manipulate the puppets on the projector stage over the background transparency.

39. *Stage or drama lighting*. In the absence of other types of lighting, use the overhead for lighting. Place colored acetates on the projector to achieve lighting effects.

40. *Costumes*. Use line drawings to visualize period costuming and how clothing has changed throughout history.

41. *Set make-up*. Use overlays to show how a set is made up of flats, platforms, and step units.

42. *Art enlarging*. Use the overhead as an art enlarger to enlarge drawings of houses, scenery, and the like. Sketch in the objects with pencil or charcoal. Then paint the flats.

43. *Floorplan*. Make a scale drawing of the stage floorplan onto a transparency. Use cut-out paper shapes made to scale to represent various furniture. Manipulate the shapes to visualize different furniture groupings.

44. *Pantomime*. Use an overhead wire to hang a large sheet on a stage. Pull the curtains until only the sheet is visible. Place an overhead projector at the back of the stage, and shine the light onto the sheet. Place players between the projector and sheet. The audience will see only silhouettes. Use in a drama class to have students act out situations.

ENGLISH (SECONDARY)

45. *Paragraph formation*. Write a series of related sentences on strips of heavy acetate. Ask students to arrange them on the projector stage to form a paragraph. Discuss possible arrangements.

46. *Composition*. Have students write a short composition or paragraph using a soft lead pencil. Run a heat copy transparency, and use it to analyze structure, grammar, spelling, and clarity.

47. *Writing styles*. Clip short articles or paragraphs from newspapers, magazines, brochures, or newsletters. Use to analyze writing styles, headline writing, and use of words.

48. *Excerpts*. Collect excerpts from good writers. Use to illustrate good writing techniques.

49. *Sentence diagramming*. Use the overhead to diagram sentences to show the relationships of words, phrases, parts of speech, and types of sentences.

50. *Explaining poetry*. Use a strip or accordion fold mask to progressively reveal a poem while explaining its meaning.

51. *Outlining*. Use a passage from a text and demonstrate how it would look in outline form. Ask students to outline a passage, using a pen and cheap plastic. Visually compare their outlines with yours.

52. *Time line*. Use a time line to visualize the period in which a particular author lived, showing who his/her contemporaries were and world events that happened during his/her lifetime.

53. *Parts of a book*. Use the overhead to visualize the parts of a book, how to break in a new book, or how to take care of a book.

54. *Student poetry*. Ask students to write poetry. Have them rewrite their poems on clear plastic; then have them explain the meaning of their poetry as the writings are projected before the class.

55. *Posters*. Use the overhead as an art enlarger to make posters about a particular book or author. Use book jackets as original artwork. Use this technique to create bulletin boards about a specific author.

56. *Word order*. Write each word of a sentence on a separate sheet of heavy plastic. Assemble the words in a number of different orders. Discuss how word order may change the meaning of the sentence.

57. *Cloze test*. Have the class use a transparency to do a "cloze" test of a passage from an assigned story.

58. *Context*. Use an overhead to show how a word can be used in various contexts and to demonstrate variations in meaning and how context determines word meaning.

59. *Parts of an essay*. Use overlays to show the parts of an essay, such as introductory paragraph, key terms paragraph, and conclusive paragraph.

60. *Extemporaneous speaking*. Write the outline of a speech onto acetate or run a heat copy transparency. Hand the transparencies to students, asking them to come project the transparency while giving a three-minute speech on its contents.

61. *Mass media*. Use advertisements clipped from newspapers and magazines to demonstrate different propaganda techniques.

62. *Correct footnotes*. Visualize examples of the correct arrangement of bibliographies and footnotes for research papers.

63. *Speech*. Use transparencies to visualize different types of speech formats, (for example, demonstration, informative, persuasive).

64. *Speech evaluation*. Use an overhead transparency to explain how to fill out a speech evaluation form.

65. *Choral reading*. Place a choral reading on a transparency. Have students read it from a screen.

66. *Satire*. Use material from magazines such as *Mad* to explain what satire is and how it is used.

67. *Compare types of poetry*. Use an overhead transparency to visually compare various forms of poetry and to compare meter.

68. *Theme requirements*. List requirements for themes (such as double-spacing, one side of the paper only, and blue or black ink). Use the list to refresh students' memories when making assignments.

69. *Card catalogue*. Use transparencies of library catalogue cards, or examples of pages from a readers' guide, to explain how to do research in the library.

70. *Shakespeare*. Use the overhead to visualize the different parts of the Globe theater and how plays were performed. Use a map of England to locate important places in Shakespeare's life.

ENGLISH
(ELEMENTARY LANGUAGE ARTS)

71. *Synonym development*. Write a sentence, such as "The man _____ across the street." Give students a small piece of clear acetate. Ask students to write a verb on the acetate. Ask them to come place it on the projector and read the sentence using their verb.

72. *Spelling words*. Place words in scrambled order. Students must unscramble them to spell them correctly. A mask system can be used to uncover the correct answers.

73. *Pronouns*. Project a transparency having pronouns and antecedents. Ask students to come to the projector and circle all pronouns and their antecedents.

74. *Crossword puzzles*. Use simple crossword puzzles to teach word meanings. Project the puzzles onto the chalkboard or butcher paper tacked to the wall. Divide the class into two teams and have them compete in completing the puzzles.

75. *Pipe cleaner animals*. Students create animals out of pipe cleaners. They lay them on the projector stage and tell about their make-believe animals.

76. *Cursive writing*. When a child has trouble forming a word or letter, write the letter on acetate and project onto the chalkboard. Have the student trace it.

77. *Comic strip sequence*. Make a comic strip into a heat copy transparency. Cut each panel, and scramble. Ask students to place the panels in correct sequence.

78. *Letter forms*. Use the overhead to visualize the form of different kinds of letters, such as personal and business letters.

79. *Verbal description*. Give pictures of animals or objects to one team of students. Ask them to describe their pictures verbally while another student tries to follow the verbal description and draw the object on the overhead.

My animal has a big body;
a small head; fat,straight legs;
and a tail at each end.

80. *Alphabetizing*. Use a transparency made from a phone book page to teach how to alphabetize.

81. *Picture dictionary*. Make a picture dictionary of words most often misused by students. Make heat copy transparencies of the dictionary. Use to review word meanings.

82. *Proofreading*. Use a transparency to explain proofreading and correction marks.

83. *Rear projection screen*. Make a rear projection screen from a cardboard box and velum paper. For children having trouble with cursive letters, project the letters and have the students trace the letters on the screen with their fingers.

84. *Word wheel*. Cut two circles of heavy acetate. Make one circle at least 2 inches smaller than the other. Write prefixes on the smaller circle. On the larger circle, write root words. Fasten circles in the center with a paper fastener. Manipulate by turning the circles to form new words.

85. *What's wrong*. Project a transparency showing sentences without capital letters and punctuation, and with incorrect spelling. Ask students to come to the projector to correct the errors.

86. *Color code parts of speech*. Write a simple sentence using different colored pens. Write the nouns in green, verbs in red, adjectives in blue, adverbs in purple, and so forth. Advance from simple to compound and complex sentences.

87. *Dictionary page*. Make a photocopy of a dictionary page or pages. Run a heat copy transparency. Underline each word that will be in larger type than the definition. Use to explain how to use the dictionary.

88. *Abbreviations and signs*. Use the abbreviation page for a transparency to explain commonly used abbreviations.

89. *Worksheet variation*. Tacktape butcher or newsprint to the classroom wall. Project a transparency of a worksheet, workbook page, crossword puzzle, or game. Ask a task force to work out the correct answers. Children enjoy this variation to doing worksheets.

90. *Cartoon dialogue*. Tacktape butcher paper or newsprint to a classroom wall. Project a transparency of a comic strip, such as Peanuts. Eliminate the dialogue in the balloons. Ask students to develop the dialogue and explain it to the class.

91. *Speech illustration*. Ask students to clip material from newspapers, magazines, brochures, and posters. Students assemble and produce transparencies to illustrate the ideas contained in a speech. Students project the transparencies when giving their speeches.

92. *Check for comprehension*. Design and produce a paragraph on a transparency. Use a mask system to uncover the paragraph for a brief time. Cover it up again and test students for comprehension.

93. *Visualize a story*. Coloring books and line illustrations from children's books are excellent artwork for children to trace onto construction plastic. Children then project the transparencies when telling stories to the class.

94. *Complete a story*. Children trace story illustrations onto cheap transparent plastic. Illustrate only half the story, up to the climax. Use the illustrations to present the story; then ask students to finish the story orally or visually.

95. *Make a filmstrip*. Cut construction plastic into long strips 10 inches wide. Draw lines to divide the strips into 10x10-inch panels. Ask each student to illustrate one panel. Roll the plastic across the projector stage while telling a story. Task forces may use this technique to make a presentation to the rest of the class.

96. *Key Words*. Write key words and names of characters from a story onto acetate. Use this to review the story. Ask students to unscramble the words and retell the story.

97. *Flannelgraph techniques*. Draw or trace a background scene onto plastic. Use heavy 7 mil acetate, such as X-ray film, cut into strips or squares. Draw or trace characters onto each piece. Manipulate the characters on the background scene while telling a story.

98. *Pick a plot*. Write ideas on a clear piece of heavy plastic, using four categories: characters, descriptions, setting, and action. Example: Farmer, wearing a fur coat, in an African jungle, played the piano. For each category, children draw illustrations on one piece of acetate. These are assembled and projected. Children are asked to tell or write a story about this plot.

99. *Matching captions*. Using handmade transparencies, the teacher tells the children a story. Each student is given a word or caption written on plastic. The teacher projects the story illustrations again. The child having the correct caption for each illustration is asked to come and place it on the projector.

100. *Mixed-up sequence*. Write, in short sentences, key actions from a story that students have either read or been told. Students are then given the sentences and asked to reconstruct the correct sequence of the story by placing the acetate strips, one by one, onto the projector.

101. *Stick figures*. Use baggies or construction plastic and felt pens. Draw stick figures to illustrate a story, story problem, or an event in history.

102. *Poetry*. Write a poem or limerick on acetate. Ask students to make up a line of the poem or limerick.

103. *Book reports*. Ask students to illustrate their book reports by tracing or drawing them on plastic. Book jackets may be used as a source of artwork.

104. *Mood music*. Play mood or contemporary music to the class. Ask students to write poems or make drawings on acetate, picturing their feelings or reactions to the music. Ask each student to present his/her poem or drawing.

105. *Film showing*. Before showing a 16mm instructional film or videotape, write key vocabulary words, main ideas, or viewing assignments. After showing the film, use the list to review or discuss the film.

MUSIC

106. *Introduction to musical instruments*. Use a transparency to visually compare the four families of musical instruments.

107. *Introduce each instrument*. Use an overhead transparency with a tape recording of an instrument to introduce each instrument to students.

108. *Melody line*. Use a mask system with a transparency of a song. Progressively uncover the musical score. Point to notes as they are being played. This idea can also be used to help students look ahead to the next notes to be sung.

109. *Note values*. Use a transparency to introduce quarter, half, and whole notes. Visualize how notes are written and their values as you play each note.

110. *Teach sight-reading*. Use a transparency of a scale to visualize how each note sound is written, and show intervals of whole and half steps. Point to each note as it is played on the piano.

111. *Biographical information*. Use maps, drawings of a composer, musical scores, and other background information on transparencies to introduce a composer to students.

112. *Time line*. Use a time line to visualize the era in which a composer lived and the contemporary composers, writers, and politicians. Tie in the composer with major events in history.

113. *Rhythm patterns*. Illustrate rhythm patterns on a transparency. Use it to beat out a rhythm being played by a k-3 rhythm and tonette band.

114. *Following directions*. Place the words of a song on a transparency. Project onto a screen or wall surface. The teacher stands beside the screen and directs. This makes it easier for students to see the conductor and the music at the same time.

115. *Rear projection screen*. Borrow or build a rear projection screen. Place colorful abstract drawings or stage scenery on transparencies. Project onto the rear projection screen while students sing or perform in front of the screen.

116. *Song illustrations*. Have students draw on acetate their ideas and feelings about a piece of music. Project the pictures on a screen beside the singing group as they sing the music. This is a good back-to-school or PTA program.

117. *Multiple images*. By making a custom frame, multiple images can be used to clarify ideas about music. For example, play a Sousa march. Place the musical notes in the main part of the transparency. In the upper left-hand corner, place a picture of the composer. In the upper right-hand corner, place a picture of the musical instrument featured in that part of the song. Manipulate the images, and point to the notes being played.

118. *Note writing*. Draw notes on a musical staff. Have students sing the notes as you write them. If they have trouble with notes or intervals, write them repeatedly. Use a water-soluble pen so that you can use the transparency over and over.

119. *Song words*. Ask students to write their own words to a song they have sung. Ask them to write their words on acetate. Project the words and have the class try to sing these words to the song.

120. *Musical parts*. Produce a transparency of a musical staff, presenting two- or three-part harmony. Use different colored notes for each part. Students then can follow their parts by concentrating on the colored note for their parts.

121. *Puppet show*. Students cut paper shapes and figures from construction paper. Play a song, such as Dance Macabre, and students use figures to act out the action or feel of the music. Several projectors and a darkened room may heighten the experience.

122. *Spotlight*. Use colored acetate sheets on the overhead to produce lighting effects for musical productions. Cut a circle in a sheet of paper to give a spotlight effect.

123. *Sound waves*. Visualize sound waves by placing the end of a tuning fork into colored water in a petri dish on the overhead stage.

124. *Quiz*. Enlarge the scope of your quizzes by asking students to identify composers, musical instruments, and songs (musical scores) placed on the overhead. For example, place a drawing of a musical instrument and ask students to identify it.

125. *Chair try-outs*. Place the music for chair try-outs on a transparency. This way, a group of judges can see the music that the student is playing, making them better able to evaluate the performance.

126. *Piano keyboard*. Divide the transparency into two parts. In the bottom half, place a drawing of the piano keyboard. At the top, write treble and base notes on a staff. Point to the note on the keyboard and as it is written on the musical score.

127. *Conducting techniques*. Use an overhead transparency and overlays to visualize each part of a conducting beat.

128. *Conducting practice*. Project a musical score onto a screen. Ask the class to practice conducting the song as you point to the notes.

129. *Finger positions*. Use transparencies to visualize the finger positions on the saxophone, clarinet, and other instruments. The teacher may stand beside the illustration on the screen with the actual instrument, demonstrating the finger positions.

130. *Assembly singing*. When the music department puts on an assembly for the student body, or a special assembly is called where students are to sing, place the words of songs on a transparency, and project onto a large screen.

ELEMENTARY MATH

131. *Counting*. Use popcorn, beans, or cut-out cardboard shapes to visualize counting from 1 to 10.

Now let's count the jelly beans... then we can eat them.

132. *Visualize addition*. Use popcorn, beans, or cut-out shapes to visualize simple addition, subtraction, and multiplication.

133. *Set theory*. Use groupings of real objects to visualize set theory. Manipulate the groupings to teach the concepts of equivalent, empty, and other sets.

134. *Quiscenaire rods*. Place quiscenaire rods on the projector stage to explain math facts. Use for review and drill.

135. *Geoboard*. Make a geoboard by drilling holes into clear plexiglass. Use golf tees for pegs. Manipulate rubberbands to teach geometric form.

136. *Abacus*. Place a small abacus on the projector stage. Manipulate it to teach addition and subtraction. It may also be used to visualize place values.

137. *Decimal placing*. Use dye-cut plastic, adhesive-backed numbers found at discount stores to create numbers. Use a dime as a decimal point. Move the dime to teach concepts relating to decimal points.

138. *Fractions*. Use circles, squares, and other geometric shapes. Cut into pieces, and manipulate the pieces to teach fractions.

How is this one-fourth of the whole?

139. *Graph grids*. Make a transparency of a graph grid. Project onto the chalkboard. Use chalk lines to plot the graph. It is easy to correct mistakes or change the graph.

140. *Teach proportion and ratio*. Draw a measure line or lines on a transparency. Project onto the wall. Students measure the line on the projector and the projected line to get a concept of proportion and ratio.

141. *More than*. Use real objects, such as popcorn or beans, to teach the concepts of "more than" and "less than."

142. *Change-making*. Use real coins on the projector stage to drill in change-making. Make a heat copy of paper money that can be used to visualize change-making.

143. *Centimeters and inches*. Use two clear plastic rulers—one in inches, the other in centimeters—to visualize the difference between the two measurements.

144. *Geometric form*. Use cut-out paper shapes of triangles, squares, and rectangles to explain how to find the area of a triangle, parallelogram, and other geometric forms.

145. *Proper and improper fractions*. Use cut-out paper shapes to visualize how to change improper fractions into proper ones. (Example: change 5/4 into 1¼).

146. *Measuring angles*. Use a transparent plastic protractor on the overhead to demonstrate how to measure an angle.

147. *Larger than/smaller than*. Use poker chips, bottle caps, beans, and other real objects to visualize the concepts of "larger than" and "smaller than."

148. *Multiplication table*. Project a multiplication table onto the wall or screen while students are working so that they may refer to it.

149. *Story problems*. Clip grocery advertising artwork. Use the artwork to make traced or heat copy transparencies that visualize components of story problems.

150. *Manipulative clock*. With a felt pen, trace around a salad plate on clear acetate. Use heavy acetate, such as cleared X-ray film. Write the numbers 1 through 12 on the clock face. Make cardboard hands, and attach them to the acetate with a paper fastener. Tape over the fastener prongs on the back of the transparency. Manipulate the hands for drill in telling time.

By moving these little hands around, you can learn to tell time...

151. *Practical math.* Use artwork clipped from magazine and newspaper advertisements to present math problems for drill in change-making. Project a problem onto the screen, and ask students how much change would be returned to the customer presenting a 10- or 20-dollar bill.

152. *Positive and negative numbers.* Use a number line on a transparency to visualize the concept of positive and negative numbers.

153. *Calculator tape.* Use a calculator tape to set up an assignment or quiz on addition or subtraction. Cut and paste up a heat copy master from the tapes. Run a heat copy transparency.

154. *Bar graph of attendance.* Assign students to make a bar graph on attendance over a given period of time. Make the graph into a transparency, and show it to the class.

155. *Grocery bill.* Use a newspaper advertisement listing grocery items and their prices. Clip and paste a problem, and make it into a transparency. You can ask students to spend a certain amount, such as $20.00, or give them items and have them figure the cost.

156. *Number facts.* To drill on number concepts, write numbers 1 through 10 on separate sheets of acetate or plastic. Have boxes of materials, such as beans, popcorn, or paper cut-outs. Place the acetate sheets on the projector stage (for example, the sheet with the number 5). A student is then asked to come place the correct number of objects on the projector stage. The rest of the class watches to see if the correct number of objects appear on the screen.

157. *Addition or subtraction.* Print simple addition or subtraction problems on separate sheets of clear acetate. Ask students to visualize the problem by placing the correct number of objects on the projector stage (for example, 3 + 3 = 6; the student would have to place three beans by each number 3). Subtraction would require the student to take away objects.

SECONDARY MATH

158. *Bell curve.* Use overhead transparencies to explain the uses of a bell curve (such as a study of populations or categories of people). Use to explain your grading of the course, if it is done on a bell curve.

159. *Slide rule.* Use the overhead to enlarge the image of a clear plastic slide rule, and explain the use of the slide rule.

160. *Theorems.* Reinforce the presentation of theorems by writing them on a clear sheet of acetate. Use the transparency to review theorems, or to compare one with another. Use drawings of complicated geometric drawings to visualize the theorems.

161. *Chalkboard geometric drawings.* More complicated geometric drawings can be placed on a transparency, projected onto the chalkboard, and traced. This can save time.

162. *Working equations.* Work equations step by step on cleared X-ray film. Use the transparency to go over the operation again, give additional remedial help after class, or for review. This saves time over the chalkboard.

163. *Probability.* Use clippings from magazines and newspapers to present problems and exercises in probability.

164. *Compass.* Use a clear plastic compass to demonstrate the measuring of angles.

165. *Student participation.* Use throw-away, cheap polyurethane plastic, such as construction plastic, sandwich bags, freezer wrap, and the like, to involve students in the solution of problems. Ask a student to come to the projector and work the problem step by step as students watch.

166. *Teaching angles.* Make a simple line drawing of a house with a triangular roof. Use the simple drawing to teach right, acute, reflex, and obtuse angles.

167. *Quiz.* Quizzes can be given on transparencies. Develop problems, and place on heat copy transparencies. Place the problems at the top, one to a transparency. Hand out the transparencies to students. Ask a student to come to the projector and solve a problem as other students watch.

168. *Mathematical symbols.* A transparency showing mathematical symbols and their definitions may be used to present the ideas to the class or to refer to while working problems.

LIBRARY SCIENCE

169. *Map of a center.* Place a map showing an instructional materials center on a transparency. When a group or class comes to work in the center, project the illustration of it to help students find what they want. The map may include the Library of Congress or Dewey numbers for each section.

170. *Library cards*. Use transparencies of library cards to explain their functions. Use the transparencies for an oral quiz on the use of the card file and library cards.

171. *Billboard*. Use the overhead and screen as a billboard to advertise new books and audiovisual materials that have recently arrived. Place the screen in a prominent place so students can see it when entering the materials center.

172. *Dewey Decimal System*. Place a chart of Dewey decimal numbers on a transparency. Use the transparency to teach the Dewey system of classification. When a group comes to work in the center, project the classification system onto a screen to help the students locate materials.

173. *Bibliographies*. Use transparencies of bibliographies to explain their correct form and use.

174. *Cross-reference*. Photocopy a page from an encyclopedia and use to explain cross-reference as used in an encyclopedia.

175. *Story hour*. Make traced or heat copy transparencies of illustrations in children's books. Mount the transparencies, and place them in a three-ring notebook. Read or dramatize the story onto cassette tape. To house the cassette, tape an envelope inside the notebook cover. Use for story hour. A student monitor may be used to start the tape recorder and place the illustrations on the projector.

176. *Back-to-school night*. Use overhead transparencies to communicate quickly the function of the materials center in the instructional program. You may want to use several projectors to project ideas, such as number of books, books on loan, amount of audiovisual materials, and equipment available. Project this information while parents browse around the center.

177. *Book care*. Use transparencies to visualize step by step how to break in a new book and how to take care of books.

178. *Library rules*. Use a transparency to explain rules in the use of the library or media center. Project the material onto a screen while a group is working in the center to remind them of the rules.

179. *Holiday materials*. Use the overhead to advertise special holiday materials. Project the information while students are working in the center.

180. *Check-out procedures*. Make transparencies of check-out cards or forms. Project the forms, and, with a water-soluble felt pen, demonstrate to students how to check out print or audiovisual materials and equipment.

181. *Special announcements or assignments*. Libraries often do not have chalkboards, but announcements and assignments for groups coming into the library can be made on the overhead.

INSERVICE FOR TEACHERS

182. *Orientation for new teachers*. Make transparencies presenting the types of services offered to the classroom teacher. Invite teachers to present their needs. Discuss how materials may be ordered.

183. *Orientation for teachers*. Make transparencies presenting any new policies or procedures that will be initiated this year.

184. *Forms*. Make transparencies of all forms used by the library or media department. Use a water-soluble felt pen to explain how to fill in each form.

185. *New equipment*. Use a transparency to explain the threading pattern for a new 16mm projector or for operational procedures for any new equipment.

186. *Promotional*. Make graphs and charts showing media materials and equipment usage for the past few years. If usage is increasing, use the diagrams to justify purchase of more equipment and materials. Emphasize any new programs you have initiated.

187. *Overhead design*. Use the guidelines presented in this book to help teachers improve their overhead transparencies. Place key words and ideas on transparencies.

188. *Student helpers*. Use a transparency while explaining to teachers, student helpers, or volunteers the duties of student helpers or volunteer help.

189. *Screen placement*. Use drawings on the overhead to discuss the correct placement of a projection screen in the classroom. Discuss angles of vision and keystoning problems.

190. *Bulletin Board*. Fasten a white sheet of paper behind overhead transparencies produced by the library or media department for teachers. Make a display of these transparencies to advertise the production services available to all teachers.

HOME ECONOMICS

191. *Table setting*. Demonstrate proper table settings by manipulating shapes of plates and utensils cut from tagboard.

192. *Recipes*. Project a recipe and ask students to multiply, divide, or change the measurements into metric equivalents.

193. *Cooking terms*. Use the overhead to visualize commonly used cooking or sewing terms and their definitions.

194. *Kitchen layout*. Draw cupboards and appliances to scale on heavy clear acetate. Cut out the shapes, and manipulate them to show possible kitchen layouts.

195. *Furniture arrangements*. Make a base cell of a room. Use cut-out tagboard shapes of furniture to visualize possible arrangements. Discuss traffic patterns.

196. *Labels*. Make heat copy transparencies of can labels to discuss contents and quality.

197. *Newspaper advertisements*. Clip newspaper advertisements and use to discuss pricing and how to obtain the best buys. You may also use the clips to discuss false advertising and advertising psychology.

198. *Bulletin boards*. Use artwork clipped from newspapers and magazines for bulletin boards. Make a heat copy transparency, and enlarge the artwork by projecting it onto poster board tacked to the wall. Trace with a felt pen.

199. *Menu planning*. Give students pieces of inexpensive plastic, such as freezer wrap, sandwich bags, or construction plastic. Ask them to plan a menu and present it to the class for discussion.

200. *Parts of a sewing machine*. Use a transparency of a sewing machine to present parts and the names of features and attachments on a sewing machine.

201. *Machine stitches*. Use a transparency to visually compare types of stitches possible with a sewing machine.

202. *Dress design*. Use transparencies and overlays to present lines of dress design and how they complement various figure types.

203. *Weaving patterns*. Use line drawings of different weaving patterns in the presentation of different types of cloth.

204. *Flower arrangement*. Use an overhead transparency in the presentation of basic principles of flower arranging.

205. *Seams*. Use a transparency and overlays to present how to sew plain, flatfilled, and french seams.

206. *Checkbook balancing*. Make heat copy transparencies of checks and balance sheets. Use to explain how to write a check and balance a checkbook correctly.

207. *House styles*. Trace basic outlines of different types of houses pictured in magazines. Make the outlines into heat copy transparencies, and use them to visually compare different styles of homes.

208. *Steam iron*. Use a transparency to explain the workings and use of the steam iron. You may also present safety precautions.

209. *Proportion*. Use the overhead to visualize the concept of proportion in dress design.

210. *Types of scissors*. Use drawings of various types of scissors to discuss correct usage.

211. *Pattern cutting*. Use a transparency to visualize how to lay a pattern on cloth so as to cut along the grain of the fabric.

212. *Cuts of meat*. Use a transparency to visualize various cuts of meat and where they are located on the carcass.

213. *Clothing expenditures*. Use graphs to visualize clothing costs and how you can save money by making your own clothes.

214. *Safety*. Visualize danger spots in the home and ideas to protect children from hazards in the home.

215. *Fundamentals of grooming*. Visually present good and bad ideas, and the basic principles of grooming.

216. *Energy management*. Visualize ideas for conserving energy in the home. Use artwork clipped from magazines and brochures.

217. *Family budget*. Visually present how to set up a budget and record-keeping.

218. *Credit*. Discuss credit and truth-in-lending and how to shop for money. Discuss how to use credit with understanding.

219. *Hand stitching*. Use the overhead to visualize the different types of hand stitches.

220. *Buttonholes*. Use a series of transparencies to explain how to make buttonholes correctly.

BUSINESS

221. *Checks*. Make and use transparencies of different styles of checks. Use the transparencies to demonstrate correct techniques for filling out a check.

222. *Bank statement*. Use a copy of a bank statement to make a heat copy transparency. Use the transparency to demonstrate how to use the statement and balance a checkbook.

223. *Income tax forms*. Use transparencies of W-2 and income tax forms to discuss how to fill out the forms. Use in conjunction with a handout.

224. *Organizational chart*. Use organizational chart transparencies to discuss management and corporate structures.

225. *Bookkeeping ledger*. Use a transparency of a bookkeeping ledger to show debits and credits.

226. *Keyboard*. A transparency of a stenograph/stenotype machine can be used to explain numbers, letters, combinations, and their uses. A transparency of a typewriter keyboard can be used to demonstrate proper finger positions and reaches.

227. *Typing speed*. Use a transparency to show how to figure words per minute in a typing test.

228. *Letter styles*. Overhead transparencies can visualize types and styles of letters. Use the transparencies to discuss form and spacing.

229. *Memo form*. Visualize how to write a memo and other inner office communication.

230. *Invoices*. Use transparencies made from purchase order and invoice forms to explain how to fill them out correctly.

231. *Title pages*. Use transparencies of sample title pages of research manuscripts to discuss spacing and how to set the pages up.

232. *Note cards*. Visualize note cards and how to prepare them for a research paper.

233. *Shorthand symbols*. Use a transparency to show how strokes are written. Use the transparency for a quiz, review, or drill. Use a mask system to reveal the correct answers.

234. *Dictation*. Have students take dictation on cheap, clear polyurethane plastic, such as construction plastic. Project some samples and ask students to correct their work. Use the samples to discuss commonly made mistakes.

235. *Job application form*. Use a transparency to demonstrate how to fill out a job application form. Use a form already filled out to discuss improper responses and how to enhance the possibility of being hired.

236. *Resume*. Use the overhead to present how to write a resume, what to include, and a sample form.

237. *Cartoons*. Cartoons clipped from magazines and newspapers can be used to teach business practices. It is a good idea to have a file. Ideas such as proper job interviewing techniques can be presented.

238. *Life insurance*. Use a graph to show the cost and savings of different types of life insurance.

239. *Interest rates*. Use a transparency to explain consumer credit and how to figure true interest rate on a loan. Use the transparency to discuss how to shop for loan money.

240. *Taxes*. Use pie charts or graphs to show where state or federal monies come from. Also, the material can be used to discuss and explain mill levies and property taxes.

241. *Newspaper headings*. Use headlines, headings, and graphic materials as a focal point in a discussion of up-to-date business trends. Use to discuss the fluctuation of the stock market.

242. *Vocations*. Use charts and graphs to present and compare vocations in business. Use graphic materials to project possible job opportunities in the future.

243. *Collection bargaining*. Use cartoons, diagrams, and charts to visualize the collective bargaining process. Use transparencies to list goals of management and labor.

244. *Balance of payments*. Use a U.S. map and diagrams to visualize expenditures (outflow) and income, or exports vs. imports. Use the material to discuss what happens when a country increases imports, decreases imports, decreases capital investment abroad, and the like.

245. *Consumer protection*. Use the overhead to visualize laws that protect the consumer, agencies that protect consumers, and procedures to take if your rights have been violated.

P. E., HEALTH, AND DRIVERS' EDUCATION

246. *Orientation*. At the beginning of the school year, use the overhead to present and reinforce an orientation to physical education (P.E.). Present activities, rules, and expectations for the year.

247. *Field day*. Use the overhead to orient students to the activities to be held on field day.

248. *Fire drill*. Use the overhead to show a map of the school to explain procedures for a fire drill.

249. *Basketball plays*. Make a transparency of a basketball court. Manipulate cut-out paper shapes, such as triangles and circles, to explain basketball plays.

250. *Announcements*. Set up an overhead projector in the gym to post special announcements for the day.

251. *Scorekeeping*. Use the overhead screen as a scoreboard for volleyball and other intramural sports.

252. *Bowling score*. Make a transparency of a bowling score sheet (or part of it) to explain how to score a bowling game.

253. *Jogging*. Use a map of the community to mark off ½, ¾, and 1 mile jogging courses. Use the overhead to present the advantages of jogging.

254. *Tumbling and diving*. Use drawings of body positions to visualize tumbling and diving positions.

255. *Caloric chart*. Use the overhead to present a caloric intake chart and how to count calories.

256. *Chess*. Use a transparency representing a chessboard and cut-out figures representing chess pieces. Manipulate the pieces to explain chess moves.

257. *X-ray*. Use an X-ray from a dentist's or doctor's office as an overhead transparency to explain teeth structure and care of teeth.

258. *Scheduling board*. Use the overhead as a scheduling board, listing what teams will play in an intramural tournament and the time schedule for games.

259. *Awards assembly*. Use the overhead at an athletic awards assembly to present team records, personal achievements, and other background information.

260. *Nutritional foods*. Clip drawings from newspapers and magazines to present good nutritional foods as opposed to "junk foods."

261. *Safety*. Use the overhead to present bicycle and sidewalk safety rules.

262. *Community hazards*. Use the overhead and a map of the community to present safety hazards found in your community.

263. *Heart and lungs*. Use an X-ray from a doctor's office and a felt pen or overlays to show the positions and functions of the heart and lungs.

264. *Grooming*. Use the overhead to visualize good grooming habits (how to brush teeth, cut fingernails, and the like).

265. *Tennis*. Use a diagram of the court, and manipulate cut-out shapes or pennies to explain player positions for tennis, volleyball, and badminton.

266. *Equipment care*. Use the overhead to reinforce explanations of equipment usage and care.

267. *Playground rules*. Use the overhead to reinforce an explanation of playground rules and specific hazards.

268. *Square dancing*. Use the overhead to explain square dance terminology and the basic steps and movements.

269. *Obstacle course*. Use the overhead to explain an obstacle course and what is done at each station.

270. *Regulatory signs*. Use materials clipped from a state driving manual to make a transparency of the shapes of signs. Use the transparency to drill students in the meaning of sign shapes.

271. *Drivers' test*. Use sample questions from a state drivers' manual to help students pass the written part of a driving test or to teach them safety concepts.

272. *Drivers' education*. Make a series of transparencies of two- and four-lane highways, intersections, and other street patterns. Use a toy car to demonstrate how to make correct lane changes, turns, and other traffic moves.

273. *Traffic penalties*. Use material from the state drivers' manual to visualize the penalties for various traffic offenses.

274. *Braking distances*. Use diagrams found in the state driver's manual to explain braking distances at various speeds.

275. *Driver's license*. Use the overhead to explain the procedure and requirements for obtaining a driver's license.

ELEMENTARY SOCIAL STUDIES

276. *Neighborhood map.* To teach elementary map reading, use the overhead with a 35mm slide projector. Project a map of the community on the overhead. Show various buildings, parks, and neighborhood scenes on a second screen, using slides. Point out on the map the location of each scene.

277. *Use with globe.* Use the overhead with a map globe to demonstrate day and night, seasons, and the like. Let the light from the projector represent the sun.

278. *Indian sign language.* Ask students to write an Indian sign language message on a transparency, and project it to see if the class can decipher it.

279. *Measuring map distances.* Use a clear plastic ruler over a transparency map to demonstrate to the class how to measure and compute distances.

280. *Shapes of states.* Trace shapes of states onto pieces of heavy acetate. Flash on the overhead and show the outlines as a game or drill in identifying states.

281. *Compare political cartoons.* Use political cartoons from different eras, such as the Civil War. Use the cartoons as a springboard for discussion. Compare a political cartoon from that era with one today.

282. *Map enlargement.* Use the overhead as an art enlarger to enlarge a state or national map onto butcher paper tacked to the wall. Use the image to plot cities, transportation, population movements, crop development, minerals, and the like.

283. *City government.* Use an organizational chart transparency to explain the function of a town or city government.

284. *World Book maps.* Use maps found in *World Book* encyclopedias to make rainfall and population and agricultural production maps.

285. *Compare size.* Trace two countries, or a country and your state, from a globe. Make one drawing into a base cell; the second into an overlay. Visualize the relative size of another state or country with your state or country. Use a globe to get the correct scale.

286. *Explain a political cartoon.* Assign students to draw a political cartoon of some current event in your state or nation. Ask students to present and explain their cartoons. Use cheap polyurethane plastics, or run a heat copy transparency of a pencil drawing.

287. *Family tree.* Use a drawing of a family tree to visualize family relationships, such as grandparents, uncles, cousins, and nieces.

288. *Mural.* Use the overhead as an art enlarger to enlarge drawings from the textbook or magazines, encyclopedias, and newspapers onto the wall to create a mural. Have children trace the outline of drawings onto cheap clear plastics, and project the outlines onto butcher paper tacked to the wall.

289. *Paper arrows and maps.* Use arrows and symbols cut from tagboard to manipulate an outline map. You can present ocean currents, pioneer routes, migrations, or battles. Cut-out paper shapes will project as a shadow or black.

290. *Viewpoints.* Use headlines or cartoons from foreign and hometown papers that refer to the same current event. Use the material to discuss why countries may have different points of view about the same event.

291. *Political viewpoints.* Clip headlines or stories from papers with different political viewpoints. Visually compare statements about the same happening. Use the material to discuss political parties or special interest groups.

292. *Historical dress.* Trace drawings from encyclopedias and history books to depict how men's and women's dress evolved from the Revolutionary War until now. Use a series of transparencies to make the visual comparison.

This is the typical American businessman of the 1980s...

293. *Concept of time*. Let 1/16 of an inch represent a year. Use a time line to visualize the length of a student's life, father's life, the oldest living person in the community, and the period of the Civil War. Start with the student's life today, and work back to the past. A 1/16th-inch scale will let you visualize up to 150 years.

294. *Vocabulary*. Use simple line drawings to illustrate the meaning of words in geography (such as peninsula, island, bay, meandering stream). Make the drawings into a type of visual dictionary. Place them in a notebook for quick access. If students fail to remember the meaning of a term, use the drawings to quickly refresh their memories.

295. *Weather map*. Clip a weather map from a newspaper, and make a heat copy transparency. Use to explain weather conditions today and weather terminology.

For the next couple of days we can expect a cloud cover...

296. *Vocabulary drill*. Use a mask to present a vocabulary drill. Uncover the correct answers to reinforce concepts.

297. *Chalkboard drawings*. Speed up the drawing of outline maps and drawings on the chalkboard by having transparencies projected onto the chalkboard. The figures can then be quickly traced.

298. *Chronological order*. Use time lines, flow charts, and other graphics to give an idea of chronological order of events in history.

299. *Script writing*. Trace or produce a series of transparencies on events in history. Project the transparencies without comment, and ask students to write a brief script about each transparency. A variation would be to have the students read the script onto a cassette tape, and then use it in a presentation to the class.

300. *Pie charts*. Trace the circumference of a saucer or pie plate onto clear plastic. Make the circle into pie charts to visualize budgets, mineral wealth, vegetable products, or industrial production of a nation.

301. *Concepts of north, south, west, and east*. On the overhead projector, place a map of the United States showing the boundaries of all states. Number the states alphabetically, beginning with Alabama as No. 1 and proceeding to Wyoming, No. 50. Make a ditto handout of the numbered states. Students must write north, south, east, or west by the name of each state.

SECONDARY SOCIAL STUDIES

302. *Visualize battle tactics*. Make transparencies of battlefields. Use simple line drawings. Cut out paper shapes to represent troups. Manipulate the shapes to progressively visualize the battle strategies. You may use this technique for naval battles, such as Midway of World War II.

303. *Sample ballot*. Make transparencies from sample ballots. You may have to divide the ballot and make several transparencies. Use to discuss candidates, issues, and amendments.

304. *Map distortion*. Visualize how maps may be distorted. Trace the outline of Greenland from a globe and a flat map. Make a base cell and an overlay to visually compare the two shapes.

305. *How a bill becomes law*. Use material found in *World Book Encyclopedia* to visualize the steps for a bill to become law. Simplify the procedure by tracing graphics that eliminate unnecessary material.

306. *Concept of distance*. When studying history or a country, give a concept of distance by comparing different places with what students already know. Use an atlas and maps of the same scale. Trace a base cell of your state, and make an overlay of the map of a region being studied. Visually compare the two. (Example: How large was the fertile crescent compared to the size of your state?)

307. *Organizational chart*. Use an organizational chart to visualize the three branches of government: executive, judicial, and legislative.

308. *Family tree*. Use a family tree diagram to visualize how European rulers intermarried and how this affected the outcome of history.

309. *Political viewpoints*. Use political cartoons to present a different view of history. (For example, our concept of Lincoln versus the sentiment of the day as portrayed by political cartoons.)

310. *Types of maps*. Visually compare the four basic types of maps: Mercator, conic, plane, and interrupted. Photocopy a sample of each type of map, and use to produce a transparency showing a sample of all four maps.

311. *Languages*. Visually compare ancient languages with English and modern language.

312. *Hieroglyphics*. Explain hieroglyphics by writing rebus words (picture writing). (Example: A picture of a bee and a leaf = belief.) Write messages for children to decipher. Ask them to construct messages.

313. *Drawing conclusions*. Project a transparency of a scene from history, an artifact, or piece of art. Ask students to study the visual and make as many conclusions as they can.

314. *Research paper*. Prepare a series of visuals on a topic, era of history, or a culture. Ask students to write a research paper explaining what they see. They may be asked to cite transparencies in the same way that they would cite a book in an ordinary research paper.

315. *Visual term paper*. Ask students to research a given topic or era in history. Ask students to visualize on cheap polyurethane clear plastic what they have found, instead of writing a research paper. They may give this visualization as a report to the class.

316. *Historical map*. Use the overhead as an art enlarger to enlarge an outline map onto butcher paper tacked to the wall. As the study of a country or history progresses, ask students to make notations of important battles, events, and persons.

317. *Old documents*. In teaching history, there is often a need to reproduce pages from old books, important documents, or historical newspapers. Using a copy machine and the heat copy process, make transparencies of the Declaration of Independence, parts of the Bill of Rights, and other documents.

318. *Headline writing*. Take a famous event in history and ask students to write a headline about the event, trying to make the headline similar to those printed in today's newspaper.

319. *Geographic terms*. The terms "longitude" and "latitude" or "parallel" and "meridian" are hard for students to understand. Use global drawings of the earth to visualize these concepts.

320. *Geography quiz*. On the projector, place a map having such features as a peninsula, bay, lagoon, or cape. Use the map to discuss vocabulary meanings. Ask students to come to the projector to label the correct feature so they can show they understand the meaning of a term (such as peninsula). Use this material as a basis for a quiz in geography.

321. *Archaeology*. Place a drawing of several artifacts on a transparency. Ask students to assume that they are archaeologists who have found the artifacts. Ask the students to make observations and conclusions about the discovery.

322. *Drill in map reading*. Produce an outline map having longitude and latitude. Place a cut-out shape of a boat or person on various spots on the map. Ask students to give the location of the figures in degrees and seconds.

323. *Size relationships*. Visualize the size of objects in history, such as pyramids, by visually comparing the objects with something already known, like a local TV tower. Use a scale drawing to make the correct comparison.

324. *Time lines*. Time line transparencies are especially useful to conceptualize time (such as the comparison of the length of the Roman Republic with the Roman Empire, or the length of our own government). Long time lines may require more than one projector projecting side by side simultaneously.

325. *Money*. Foreign and U.S. paper money generally will reproduce on heat copy transparency material. The transparencies can be used to compare size and types of paper money, including Confederate, or to compare foreign currencies.

326. *Television visuals*. When doing classroom television production, the overhead is a good source of graphics. Maps, charts, cartoons, quotations, and illustrations may be projected onto the screen and videotaped. Special effects may be obtained by using overlays and mask systems.

327. *Opinion poll*. Have students take an opinion poll on some current issue in your community. Have students translate their results into charts and graphs. Ask students to make transparencies of the graphs and present their findings to the class.

ELEMENTARY SCIENCE

328. *Astronomy*. Punch holes in a sheet of tagboard to represent stars and planets. Use photographs or diagrams of the heavens to guide you. Project onto a screen, or turn out the lights and project onto the ceiling.

329. *Centigrade and Fahrenheit*. Use drawings of the two different thermometer scales. Visually compare the two. Use the drawings to discuss freezing and boiling points on each scale.

330. *Seed sprouting*. Use four overlays to progressively show the germination of a seed. Overlays should show: 1) the seed, 2) rootlet, 3) sprouting shoot and young root system, 4) the growing stem, early foliage, and spreading roots.

331. *Chemical reactions*. Simultaneously place small strips of aluminum in three petri dishes. In dish one, place hydrochloric acid; dish two, sodium hydroxide; and dish three, nitric acid. Place the dishes on the overhead stage so the whole class can see the reactions.

332. *Camera shutter speed*. Demonstrate shutter speeds for an elementary photography course by placing a lens from a view camera on the projector stage. Manipulate the shutter and f-stop mechanism.

333. *Animal observation*. Place polliwogs, tadpoles, or fish in a transparent bowl or dish. Let students observe the animals' movements on the screen. Place a colored sheet of acetate on the projector stage to cut down glare.

334. *Insects*. Place insects in a petri dish and let children observe their movements on the screen.

335. *Animal tracks*. Use the overhead to compare the shape and size of animal tracks. Use this presentation for a game or quiz. Ask students to identify the animal by its track.

336. *Magnetic attraction*. Place iron filings in an envelope made from two clear sheets of acetate taped together on all four sides. Manipulate the magnet, placing the iron filings onto the projector stage. Students can see magnetic attraction by the movement of the filings.

337. *Electrical circuitry*. Develop wiring diagrams on the overhead. Start with a partially prepared transparency. Use a felt-tipped pen to fill in the missing circuits.

338. *Weather map*. Make a transparency from a weather map obtained from the U.S. Weather Bureau. Ask students to take an imaginary journey. Ask them what kinds of weather conditions they would encounter. Use the map to teach vocabulary.

339. *TV production*. Use transparencies of weather maps as background material for in-class videotaping. Ask students to do a newscast, weather report, or sportscast. Use the transparencies as visual and background material.

340. *Leaves*. Place leaves in an envelope made of two sheets of clear acetate taped on all four edges. Use double-edged tape to mount the leaves in place. Use this material to discuss types of trees. The leaves will project as a shadow or black.

341. *Wave motions*. Demonstrate wave motion of sound by placing a tuning fork in a shallow transparent dish filled with colored water. Place the dish on the overhead stage.

342. *Compass demonstration*. Clear Plexiglas compasses are marketed and may be used on the projector stage to enlarge the compasses for the class to observe. Use this demonstration to explain compass use and vocabulary (such as southeast and northwest).

343. *Gear ratio*. Mount toy gears or real gears from a machine onto a clear piece of Plexiglas. Ask students to count how many times the small gear rotates to one revolution of the big gear. Use this demonstration to discuss gear ratio.

344. *X-rays*. Discarded X-rays may be obtained from doctors' offices, hospitals, and X-ray labs. Use the X-rays to explain bone structure of different parts of the body.

345. *Thermometer*. Remove the bulb and stem of a thermometer from a wooden backing. Mount the bulb and stem onto a clear Plexiglas backing. Project this form when discussing thermometer readings. Use a match or ice to discuss how to read the thermometer.

346. *Barometer*. Use a drawing of a barometer in conjunction with a real one to explain how the barometer works. Use this material to explain rising and falling barometers.

347. *Student reports.* There is a wealth of science material in an encyclopedia. Give students sandwich bags (or other cheap clear plastic) and ask them to trace illustrations; use the illustrations to make research reports to the rest of the class. Use water-soluble felt pens to trace the drawings.

348. *Climactic zones.* Divide the transparency into two parts. On the left, make a drawing of a mountain peak; on the right, a sea shore and ocean. Use the transparency to explain the different climactic zones and how elevation affects climate. It may also be used to explain water cycles, evaporation, condensation, and precipitation.

349. *Observational skills.* Use this transparency to help students develop accurate observation, classification, and record-keeping. At the top of the transparency, write the name of the experiment. Draw a line down the center, dividing the transparency into two parts. On the left, place the heading "Differences." On the right, place the heading "Similarities." Fill in the two sides as children make their observations of a scientific experiment.

350. *Scientific method.* Teach hypothesizing. Divide the transparency into two equal parts by drawing a line across the center. At the top of the transparency, write "What we thought." At the top of the bottom half, write "What we learned." Draw lines to guide you in writing the observations. Ask students to make a hypothesis. After an experiment, ask students to test their hypothesis.

351. *Environmental puppet show.* Use felt-tipped pen lines and colored acetate sheets to create a background environment (such as the sea). Make traced drawings of birds or animals onto heavy strips of clear acetate. Students manipulate the drawings while discussing the animals' diet, habits, and enemies.

352. *Photosynthesis.* Use a diagram of a leaf and stem to explain photosynthesis and terms such as "oxygen," "sugar," "chlorophyll" and "CO_2."

353. *Heart action.* The pumping action of the heart and blood circulation can be visualized using special sheets of polarized material and a polarized spinner.

SECONDARY SCIENCE

354. *Electrical circuitry.* Demonstrate a circuit and electrical flow by using a polarized spinner on the projector lens and polarized material on the transparency.

355. *Micrometers.* Enlarge a demonstration for the class to observe by manipulating the micrometer on the overhead projector stage. Opaque objects will project as a shadow or black.

356. *Exchange of atoms.* Visualize the exchange of atoms in reversible equations by manipulating transparent colored acetate disks with a rubber pencil eraser.

357. *Solutions.* On the projector stage, demonstrate color changes of various chemical indicators by adding the indicators to weak acid and base solutions in shallow petri dishes.

358. *Chemical formulas.* Write, or progressively reveal, explanations of complex chemical formulas. Encourage the class to work with you. Use this material for review or to help students who have been absent.

359. *Food chain.* A good method of presenting the idea of a food chain is to use simple drawings or flowcharts on a transparency.

360. *Photographic transparencies.* A local offset printer can make a negative photograph of any illustration. Generally, the illustration can be enlarged from 2 to 300% or reduced from 20 to 30% of the original size. The negative will project as a transparency.

361. *Experiments.* Vertical positioning of experiments in front of the 12x12-inch projector stage is possible by laying the projector on its side. Lay the projector head down away from the screen.

362. *Lab assignments.* Distribute a handout to students working on a lab assignment. Use a transparency to explain step by step the lab procedure written on the handout. You may also explain behavioral objectives.

363. *Classification.* Help students develop accurate observation and note-keeping skills. At the top of a transparency, write the name of the specimen or experiment. Divide the transparency into two parts by drawing a line down the center. Label the left half "Similarities." Label the right half "Differences." A student then uses the transparency to lead a discussion or report to the class.

364. *Overhead transparencies from slides.* Use a single lens reflex camera and close-up lenses to photograph an insect or picture from a book. Project the slide onto typing paper tacked to a wall. Trace the image with a soft lead pencil. Simplify or add captions to the illustration as necessary. Run as a heat copy transparency.

INDUSTRIAL ARTS

365. *Tool identification*. Use simple line drawings to help students identify each tool and its function. Use the drawings in a quiz to test comprehension.

366. *Safety regulations*. Use the overhead to project safety rules while you explain them. Use the transparency to review safety rules periodically.

367. *Correcting mechanical drawings*. Design mechanical drawing assignments so that an overhead transparency can be laid over it. You can immediately see mistakes in the drawing.

368. *Clean-up assignments*. Write the names of those who are on clean-up detail each day. Project the list at the end of each class so that students are reminded who is to clean up.

369. *Project grading criteria*. So students understand the requirements for a grade, use a transparency to visualize the grading criteria for each project.

370. *Vocabulary*. Use the overhead to visualize vocabulary that you are presenting. This helps students to understand how to spell each word.

371. *Bolt threads*. Use an overhead transparency to visualize the different types of bolt threads.

372. *Measuring*. Use a clear plastic ruler on the overhead to demonstrate correct methods of measuring (for example, how to measure a cut in a board correctly).

373. *Board feet*. Use the overhead to present how to figure board feet. On a clear sheet of acetate, demonstrate step by step how to figure board feet.

374. *Machine parts*. Use transparencies and overlays to explain parts of a machine and how they function. For example, visualize the parts of a wood plane, how it is assembled and adjusted.

375. *Safety devices*. Use drawings of machine safety devices when discussing the devices and their function.

376. *Foundry procedures*. Visualize foundry procedures and sand casting techniques. Use overhead transparencies in conjunction with real objects (castings).

377. *Tool sharpening*. Use the overhead to visualize the correct techniques for sharpening tools.

378. *Nail sizes*. Visualize the size and shape of different types of nails by laying them on the projector stage, or use transparent tape to affix them to a clear sheet of plastic.

379. *Types of wood joints*. Visually compare the different types of joints and vocabulary associated with them.

380. *Electrical circuits*. Make a transparency of an electrical circuit. Use the transparency to explain basic wiring of a house. Negative transparencies work well in explaining circuitry.

381. *Battery*. Visualize the components of a battery and how they operate. Contrast wet and dry cells.

382. *Leather working*. Use the overhead to present different types of leather tools and their operation. Visualize tooling processes and lacing techniques.

383. *Perspective*. Use simple line-drawing transparencies to teach perspective as used in mechanical drawing.

384. *Sheet metal work*. A pattern must be developed before any job can be cut out of sheet metal. Use the overhead to visualize the methods of developing a pattern. Use the transparency for review and to give out-of-class help to students.

385. *Wood framing vocabulary*. It would be difficult to explain the terms joist, header, rafter, plate, and studs without a drawing. The overhead offers a way to present complicated drawings too difficult to draw on the chalkboard.

386. *Types of roofs*. Use the overhead to visually compare the construction of different types of roofs, such as hip and gable.

387. *Job opportunities*. Clip advertisements from the newspaper and make them into a heat copy transparency to present vocational opportunities.

388. *Cartoons*. Comic strips and cartoons can often be used to present situations relating to industrial arts. Use these materials to add interest to a presentation or lecture. You can relabel or caption the cartoon to give a local application.

389. *History and philosophy*. Use cartoons and simple line-drawing transparencies to present the history and philosophy of industrial arts. Use the transparencies to motivate students to sign up for industrial arts courses.

SKILL DEVELOPMENT

KINDERGARTEN

390. *Body concept.* Help children improve their concept of their bodies in space. Draw a map or picture of the movements that children are to make. Have them translate the drawing into movements.

391. *Wire sculpture.* Fine motor coordination may be developed through wire sculpture. A child must complete a motor-driven pattern to create a sculpture. Children bend soft pliable wire to resemble animals or objects. Have them present their animal to the class by laying it on the overhead projector stage.

392. *Hand shadows.* Use the lamp on an overhead projector to provide a beam of light. Children use their fingers to make shadow patterns of circles, triangles, squares, and animal shapes on the wall. Have each child talk about the animals he/she makes.

393. *Developing directionality.* Help children develop directionality by printing symbols onto a sheet of clear plastic. Symbols, such as an *E*, may be made to face left, right, up, or down. Ask children to point their hand in the same direction as the *E* or symbol.

394. *Directionality problems.* For a child who reverses letters or words, print them on clear acetate and project onto the chalkboard. Have children trace the letter or word on the chalkboard.

395. *Pick a stunt.* Teach body parts, word recognition, and basic skill practice by printing verbs onto pieces of heavy acetate. Place the pieces into a box. Have a child draw out a verb, such as "*raise* arms over your head," or "*clasp* hands." The class then performs the action presented on the piece of acetate.

396. *Visual discrimination.* Make a type of bingo game card by dividing a piece of cardboard into nine small squares. Mark a different letter of the alphabet on each square. Write the 26 letters of the alphabet on clear acetate squares. Have children draw, one at a time out of a box, one of the 26 alphabet letters. Place the letter on the overhead projector for the class to see. Students check their cards, and place a small cardboard square over the letter on their card that matches the one on the projector. The first student to get three covered squares in a row is the winner.

397. *Same and different drill.* From workbooks, trace onto strips of clear acetate four small objects that are the same and one that is different (example: four balls and one square). Project the drawings on the overhead onto a rear projection screen. Ask students to come and point or touch the object that is different.

398. *Visual memory strips.* Make a set of 15 memory strips by writing four letters of the alphabet on each strip of clear acetate. The letters should not form words (example: M B O Z). Briefly project the letters onto the screen, and ask students to write down the sequence on scrap paper.

399. *Animal identification.* Trace animal drawings onto heavy pieces of clear acetate. Use this material to help students identify the name of each animal. Ask students to classify the animals according to where they live—in a zoo, farm, or house.

400. *Teach colors.* Use wide-tipped felt pens and pieces of heavy clear acetate. Make a circle of color on each piece of acetate. Use this material to visualize colors and to contrast or compare colors.

401. *Alphabet.* Cut out shapes of letters from tagboard or use die cut letters. Flash the letters onto the screen, asking children to identify each one.

402. *Match the baby.* Trace pictures of the mother and baby animals onto heavy clear acetate. Ask students to match the correct baby with its mother.

403. *Identify parts of the body.* Use traced drawings on heavy clear acetate to present and drill students on the parts of the body. Draw arms, legs, head, and body onto separate sheets of acetate.

404. *Safety signs.* Trace different traffic signs from a page out of the state drivers' manual. Project the material and use to teach what signs and signals mean. Use to teach sidewalk safety.

405. *Calendar.* Copy a calendar sheet of a particular month onto an overhead transparency. Use the transparency to designate important dates and holidays. Write "Happy Birthday" in the date square for children having birthdays on that date.

406. *Animal puppets.* Cut out the body, head, and legs of an animal, such as a horse. Fasten the body parts together with paper fasteners. Place the figure on the projector stage, manipulating the legs, tail, or head as you tell a story.

407. *Counting.* Manipulate real objects, such as popcorn, beans, or cardboard shapes, to teach counting from 1 to 10. Place objects onto the projector stage as the students count, or use the objects for drill.

408. *Traced transparencies*. Trace line drawings from coloring or children's storybooks. This presentation is especially good for holiday stories. Punch the acetate sheets with a three-hole notebook punch, and place the sheets into three-ring notebooks. Place drawings on the projector as you tell the story.

PRIMARY ELEMENTARY

409. *Introduce new vocabulary*. Take new words from the basal reader and present them to the class on the overhead. Use this method to present meaning, pronunciation, and inflection.

410. *Heading on papers*. Students often fail to place the proper heading on their papers. Use a transparency visualizing the correct heading. Ask students to copy it onto their papers.

411. *Quiscenaire rods*. Use Quiscenaire rods on the projector stage to visualize math concepts. Transparent Quiscenaire rods may be made from Plexiglas or colored acetate.

412. *Blends*. Write a three-letter combination, such as Str, on a piece of clear acetate. On a strip of acetate, write possible word endings, such as eam, ong, aight, etc. Manipulate the material to teach two- and three-letter combinations.

413. *Read and do*. Make a list of directions you give repeatedly to your class. Write them on a sheet of clear acetate. Instead of giving oral instructions, turn on the overhead for a change of activity. Get attention by flicking the projector on and off. If a child doesn't understand, go over to him/her and point to a student who is doing what the visual says. (Suggested messages might include: Stop work; Clear your desk; Get out milk money.)

414. *Study spelling transparency*. Write the following rules for studying spelling: Look at the word; Hear the word; Say the word; Close your eyes and "see" the word; Write the word, Check the word. Use these rules with each spelling lesson.

415. *Sentence order*. Write a sentence on heavy clear acetate. Cut the sentence into pieces. Ask students to assemble the material into a sentence. Use this method to discuss word order.

416. *Money*. Make a heat copy transparency of 1-, 2-, 5-, 10-, 20-, and 50-dollar bills. Photocopy coins and make heat copy transparencies. Use this transparency to explain our money system.

417. *Lower-case and capital letters*. Cut out the alphabet from tagboard or use die cut letters. You must have a complete set of upper- and lower-case letters. Ask students to come to the projector and correctly match the lower-case letter with the equivalent capital letter.

418. *Set theory*. Use real objects, such as beans or popcorn and pieces of yarn, to teach set theory. Encircle objects with the yarn to form sets.

419. *Telling time*. Make a clock face by tracing the circumference of a salad plate. Write in clock numbers with a felt pen. Stick a thumbtack from the back side of the clock face through the center. Make and stick on tagboard hands. Place a small eraser on the point of the thumb tack to hold hands in place. Manipulate the hand for drill in telling time.

420. *Bigger than*. Teach the concepts of "bigger than," "smaller than," "largest," "smallest," by using large and small shapes cut from tagboard. Manipulate the shapes on the projector stage.

421. *Emotions*. Using cartoon characters, such as Charlie Brown, visualize different emotions. Use this presentation to stimulate discussion of emotions.

422. *Seating chart*. Make a transparency of the seating chart. Use the transparency to introduce a new seating arrangement or for dividing the class into study groups.

423. *Halloween story*. Create a spooky atmosphere in the classroom. Darken the room if possible. Place a plastic dish with colored water in it onto the projector stage. While reading a Halloween story, drop Alka Seltzer in the water for a special effect.

424. *Observational skills*. Produce a series of transparencies having unrelated illustrations, such as dogs, toothbrushes, flowers, toys, and the like. Flash the illustrations onto the screen, and ask students to list as many items as possible. Turn on the projector to check answers.

425. *Safety*. Draw a map of the neighborhood on a sheet of clear acetate. Use toy cars and cardboard shapes representing people to visualize hazards in the community. Use this material to present safety problems, and ask students to solve them by coming to the projector and manipulating the objects.

426. *Yellow pages*. Make transparencies of the yellow pages to help students learn how to use the yellow pages and the telephone.

UPPER ELEMENTARY

427. *Map symbols*. Enlarge map symbols found on maps. Draw the symbols on clear acetate, and use them to explain or quiz students on the meaning of these symbols.

428. *Introduce bar graphs*. Use a felt-tipped pen and masking tape to create simple bar graphs. Make the grid with the pen, and cut masking tape to length to form the bars.

429. *Field trip*. Write the things students are to look for while on a field trip. The teacher may make a simple map to help orient students to the scene. Use the transparency to make observational assignments or to review what students have seen during the field trip.

430. *Present a 16mm film*. Use a handmade transparency to introduce a 16mm film. Make viewing assignments by writing them on the transparency. Write the name of students beside each assignment. Use this material to discuss what students have seen.

431. *Visualize a film*. Ask students to make drawings to illustrate what they have seen in a film or filmstrip. Run the film without the picture, or play the filmstrip recording while the students project their visuals.

432. *Film vocabulary*. Write vocabulary words new to students on a sheet of clear acetate. Write word meanings. Use this material for review after showing the film.

433. *Special greetings*. Ask students to make special welcoming messages for new students, students who have been ill, or for birthdays. Project the greetings when the student enters the class.

434. *Rules of conduct*. Use the overhead to reinforce and explain rules of conduct. Use the material for a quick review if a rule has been broken.

435. *Video graphics*. Projected overhead transparencies of drawings, maps, charts, graphs, and other graphics may be used in a student-produced video-tape. A form of animation can be obtained by manipulating overlays or pieces of acetate.

436. *Tell-the-truth game*. Write three to five statements on a subject being studied. Project the statements and ask students to decide which statements are true and which ones are false.

437. *Riddles*. Project a riddle. Divide the class into teams. See which group can solve the riddle first. Give points for each correct answer.

438. *Secret code messages*. Scramble words or use a code system. Write a message on a transparency and have students decode it. The message may be a special announcement you want students to understand.

439. *Math baseball*. Draw a baseball diamond on a piece of clear acetate. Use cut-out tagboard shapes to represent players. Use drill cards on any subject, such as multiplication tables. Easy questions are a base hit; harder ones are a double; very hard questions, a home run. A missed question is a strike out. Divide the class into two teams. The winner is the team with the most runs after all students have had a turn.

440. *Crossword puzzle*. Use simple crossword puzzles to teach word meanings. You may want to make your own puzzle, using vocabulary words for this week. Divide the class into two teams. Project the puzzle and see which group can correctly solve it first.

441. *Game rules*. Place the rules of games or game boards on an overhead transparency. Project the rules while students are playing the game so they may quickly refer to them.

442. *Tic-tac-toe*. Draw the tic-tac-tie grid on a sheet of clear acetate. Divide the class into two teams, one representing *o*'s, the other *x*'s. Each participant can choose where to put an *x* or *o* before a question is asked. If the student correctly answers the question, the *x* or *o* is written on the grid. Play as many games as necessary until each student has had a turn. The team with the most points is the winner.

443. *Brainstorming session*. Use the overhead as a focal point of a brainstorming session. Write each idea as students present them. Use the material later to evaluate ideas.

444. *Discussion*. Write the main ideas presented in a discussion. Use the material to review or sum up arguments on an issue.

445. *Introduce a unit of study*. Use a transparency to introduce the main ideas to be studied in a unit of study. Use the transparency later for review of the unit.

446. *Sandwich bag transparencies*. Ask students to trace pictures or write on cheap plastic, such as sandwich bags, construction plastic, or freezer wrap. Students use the transparencies to report their research to the class.

447. *A day at school*. Ask students to draw their ideas of a day at school on clear acetate. They may dramatize or narrate their ideas onto a cassette tape. Use the material for a program at PTA or Back-to-School night.

448. *Correcting quizzes.* Write the answers to a quiz, or make an overlay so that students can quickly correct their own papers.

449. *Motivation.* Place a cartoon on the overhead as students enter the classroom in the morning. The cartoon may be a "sunshine" message or humorous. It may present some special event that is going to happen that day.

450. *Sign making.* Rub dry transfer (rub-on) letters onto clear acetate, spelling the sign message. Project the message onto poster board, a banner, or plywood. Trace the letters with a soft pencil. Color the letters with felt pens or tempora paint.

451. *Slide projector.* If a slide projector is not available, slides may be shown on the overhead. Make a cardboard frame, cutting out a window just large enough for the slide. Place the slide in the window and project onto the screen. Move the projector farther away from the screen to enlarge the image.

452. *Slide sorter.* The overhead makes an excellent light table or slide sorter. Place a sheet of white paper on the projector stage.

453. *Super Bowl spelling.* Project a transparency of a football field with the yard lines marked from 10 to 50. Place spelling words into a coffee can. Divide the class into two teams. Place a cut-out paper shape of the ball on the 50 yard line. A member of one team draws a spelling word and pronounces the word. A member from the opposite team must spell the word. If the word is spelled correctly, the ball is advanced 10 yards. If the student misspells the word, the ball is moved back 10 yards. The first team to get their ball over the goal line makes a touchdown. Students may play the game until the spelling words are all gone.

454. *Teleprompter.* Place a dialogue to be used in a classroom TV production onto a transparency, and project it onto a screen where it can be easily read by student actors. Assign a student to point to the dialogue if another student gets stuck and to change transparencies as the dialogue progresses.

FOREIGN LANGUAGE

455. *Visual information.* Use the overhead projector in a language lab to present visual information, such as spelling or vowel sounds, while remaining seated at the control console.

456. *Verb endings.* Place verb stems on one sheet of acetate. Place overlays over the base cell, showing verb endings. This is effective in grouping types of stems that use different endings.

457. *Word pictures.* Help students remember new vocabulary through pictures instead of using the English word translation. Use pictures of objects or activities with the proper vocabulary. Drill by using mask systems to flash objects quickly on the screen.

458. *Telephone book.* Use pages out of a foreign city telephone book for a presentation and drill on how to use the phone.

459. *Imaginary trip.* Use illustrations and advertisements from a foreign newspaper to make an imaginary trip to a department store, food market, or theater. Use this material as a motivator to stimulate conversation.

460. *Traffic signs.* Use drawings of various traffic signs to stimulate conversation and vocabulary drill.

461. *Dictation.* If you give dictation in a foreign language, use a transparency to help students correct their papers. Immediate feedback can be helpful.

462. *Telling of time.* Use a transparency of a clock face with movable cardboard hands (see Elementary Math) to drill in the telling of time in a foreign language.

463. *Comic strips.* Make transparencies of foreign comic strips. Cut out parts of the dialogue, and ask students to respond and complete the dialogue.

464. *Foreign money.* Some foreign paper money will reproduce on the heat copy process. Use the transparency to present the money system of a country and how to make change.

465. *Political cartoons.* Make transparencies of political cartoons from a country being studied. Use the transparencies to explain the problems and culture of that country.

466. *Crossword puzzles.* Use crossword puzzles in a foreign language to drill in a language or as a fun game to develop vocabulary concepts.

467. *Panoramic view.* Write conjugations and verb tenses on a series of transparencies. Use these transparencies to show where each lesson fits into the whole pattern of the language.

468. *Descriptive exercise.* Use transparencies of action drawings or situations. Ask students to describe the action or situation orally. This is a good exercise to develop usage of adjectives and adverbs.

469. *Songs*. Help students learn the words to songs from the country they are studying. Place song words on a transparency, and use the transparency when singing the song or when playing a disk recording.

470. *Poetry*. Place the words of a poem on the overhead while playing a recording of a native speaker reading the poem. Use this material to discuss pronunciation, inflection, and rhythm.

471. *Postcard*. As a variation to written work in a foreign language, make a drawing of a postcard on clear acetate. It should include the stamp, lines for the address, and a space for the message. Ask students to imagine they are in a foreign country and are writing a postcard home to their parents or friends. After they have written the message, ask them to project it on the overhead, sharing it with the class.

IDEAS FOR USING MATERIALS FROM NEWSPAPERS AND MAGAZINES

The newspaper is one of the inexpensive resources readily obtainable in almost any community. Here are some ideas on using graphic materials found in newspapers and magazines. Clip and paste up heat copy transparencies.

472. *Headlines*. Project a transparency of a newspaper headline. Ask students to write a news story relating to the headline.

473. *Political advertisements*. Make a transparency from advertisements obtained from opposing political candidates. Use the material to discuss issues, mudslinging, misleading statements, and other political concepts.

474. *Political cartoon*. Use a political cartoon to discuss current public reaction to an event. Ask students to use pencils to draw their own political cartoon. Make a transparency of select drawings, and ask students to explain their feelings.

475. *Old political cartoons*. Obtain old political cartoons by going to a newspaper office to get old newspapers, if they are available, or by using the paper's library. Use the cartoons to compare public opinion then and now.

476. *Free offer advertisement*. Make a transparency of a free offer advertisement. Use the transparency to discuss misleading advertisements, what the advertising is seeking, and the like.

477. *Real estate advertisement*. Use a real estate advertisement to stimulate discussion on percentage. Ask students to figure the commission of a salesman, interest rate on a loan, and rates of depreciation or appreciation.

478. *Savings advertisement*. Use an advertisement from a savings and loan association or bank to discuss interest rates, how to shop for the best interest rates, and how to figure interest on a savings account. Use this material with a unit on consumer credit.

479. *Store advertisements*. Use advertising to visualize story problems and make problems more relevant to students. Give students a grocery list, and ask them to spend an amount of money at the store by selecting items from the advertisement.

480. *Menu planning*. Use grocery advertisements to discuss best buys and menu planning.

481. *Inflation*. Ask students to keep grocery advertisements in a notebook over a period of a school year. Students should date each advertisement as it is placed into the notebook. Students may then compare the cost of items throughout the school year to see the effect of inflation on the cost of products.

482. *Movie advertisements*. Use movie advertisements to stimulate students to read the books from which the motion picture was made. Advertisements can also be used in book reports.

483. *Fashion advertisements*. Use artworks in fashion advertisements to discuss clothing design and fashion trends. Compare current dress patterns with those of the past.

484. *Help wanted advertisements*. Use the want advertisements to stimulate a role-playing situation. Have students role-play a job interview. Videotape the interview, and use the tape to critique the student's demeanor.

485. *Auto advertisement*. Project an auto advertisement onto the screen, and use it to stimulate language development. Ask students to telephone an inquiry, write a letter about the advertisement, or write their own advertisement for an automobile. The advertisement can be used to stimulate many types of role-playing activities.

486. *Newspaper advertisement of their own*. Ask students to write an advertisement to sell their most personal possession. Have students write the advertisement on clear plastic and present it to the class. Use this presentation to stimulate oral expression by having someone respond to the advertisement.

487. *Weather map*. Project a weather map from a newspaper, and use it to discuss weather conditions and concepts such as centigrade, fahrenheit, and barometric pressure.

488. *Radio/TV section*. Use a transparency of a radio/TV schedule to explain a viewing assignment. Use advertisements for a TV program in the Sunday section of the newspaper when discussing the plot and characters.

489. *Cartoons*. Clip cartoons from a newspaper or magazine. Make the cartoons applicable to a local situation by adding your own captions and labels. Ask students to use the cartoons and the overhead when making speeches.

490. *Graphic design*. Clip artwork from newspapers and magazines to teach the use of type and graphic design. Use advertisements as models, and ask students to design their own advertisements using principles of design found in the transparency.

491. *Propaganda*. Use advertisements and artwork from newspapers and magazines when discussing propaganda, truth-in-lending laws, consumer protection laws, and the like.

492. *Environmental studies*. Use transparencies of headlines and articles on environmental problems in your community as a springboard to a discussion on the environment. Ask students to evaluate statements made in a biased article on an environmental problem.

493. *Visual dictionary*. Cut out letters of the alphabet from headlines. Cut out drawings of objects beginning with each letter of the alphabet. Assemble the material and make into transparencies. Project the transparencies to introduce or review letters of the alphabet.

494. *Vocational study*. Use help wanted advertisements to explore vocational possibilities and current demand for a vocation. Use transparencies of advertisements to stimulate the study of a vocation.

495. *Colloquialisms and slang expressions*. Use transparencies made from comic strips or cartoons to explain sayings, colloquialisms, or slang expressions. Use to teach commonly used expressions in a foreign language.

496. *Self-esteem*. Use a stamp pad and clear acetate to make thumbprints of the students in your class. Project the transparency and discuss how each student is unique and different from every other person and is thus important. Use to build self-esteem.

497. *Lost and found*. Project a lost and found advertisement by making a heat copy transparency. Ask students to write a short story about what they think might have happened to cause the loss. Ask them to draw pictures to illustrate their stories. Have students draw onto sandwich bags or cheap plastics. Then ask students to share their stories with the class, projecting their illustrations while they tell the stories.

498. *Temperature graph*. Assign students to check the temperatures around the nation as recorded in newspapers found in the library. Then ask students to make a transparency of the graph, plotting the warmest spot, coldest spot, and local temperatures. Students can project the graph while explaining their findings.

499. *Abbreviations*. Make a transparency of a section in the want advertisements that has a number of abbreviations. Project the abbreviations, and ask students to figure out their meanings.

500. *Antonyms*. Select an advertisement from a magazine or newspaper that has many descriptive words praising a product (such as fresh, crisp, crunchy, juicy). Make the advertisement into a transparency, and project. Ask students to rewrite the advertisement using words that mean exactly the opposite of those used in the advertisement. Students may then read their advertisements to the class.

501. *Where is it*? Project a map of the United States, including outlines of the states and key cities on it. Ask students to look at news reports in the newspaper. Ask them to find where the news took place and to point to the location on the map. This is a fun way to test on the location of states and cities.

Appendix 1

Glossary of Terms

Acetate. *See* Clear acetate.

Aperture. The opening (generally 7½x9½ inches) through which the projection light passes on an overhead transparency mount.

Artwork. Any graphic material, either printed or handmade, such as drawings, illustrations, and photographic reproductions.

Base cell or cel. The acetate taped to the back of a transparency mount. It may be a sandwich of several acetate sheets.

Black line transparency. A black line image on a clear or tinted acetate sheet. Used in the heat copy process.

Carbon ink. A black ink containing pigment of Lampblack (or other carbon) used in drawing ink or printer's ink. Necessary for creating masters in the thermo copy process.

Clear acetate. An all-purpose transparent cellulose plastic sheet used much like an ordinary sheet of paper for drawing or writing, having a surface which will accept markings from felt pens.

Color adhesive. Adhesive-backed transparent or translucent color printed on thin acetate. It is available in sheet or tape form.

Colored line transparencies. A specific type of acetate transparency that yields a colored line when run through the thermographic (heat) process. Usually has an activator sheet to activate the dye.

Dry transfer letters. Transparent colored or opaque black letters available in assorted styles, sizes, and colors which are printed on a plastic sheet and transferred to any dry surface by burnishing the letter with a blunt instrument.

Faxable. Artwork and printed matter containing carbon and capable of reproduction, using the heat copy process.

Felt-tip or -tipped pen (nonpermanent). A pen having a water-base ink available in many colors and assorted points.

Felt-tip or -tipped pen (permanent). A pen similar to the above except it contains permanent ink which cannot be removed with water.

Frame. *See* Overhead transparency mount.

Graphics. *See* Artwork.

Grease pencil. A nonpermanent crayon-like material in pencil form for writing on acetate.

Halftone. Artwork which consists of a gradation of tones, such as a photograph as compared with black-and-white line drawings.

Heat copy transparency material. *See* Heat-sensitive acetate.

Heat-sensitive acetate. Acetate coated with a dye actuated by heat (infrared) and used in making heat copy transparencies.

Keystone effect. A projected image which is wider at the top than at the bottom or wider on one side than on the other side because the light beam from the projector lens is not an equal distance to the top and bottom of the screen.

Keystoning. *See* Keystone effect.

Layout. The arrangement and form of the various aspects of illustrative and printed matter.

Layout sheet. Paper having the outline of the overhead transparency aperture drawn on it and used in designing transparency masters.

Leading edge. The edge of the layout sheet that will enter the thermocopy machine first.

Light table. A frosted glass-surfaced table having a light source beneath the glass and used by graphic artists.

Line drawings. Drawings in which there are no grays and in which texture is obtained with black and white lines or dot patterns.

Mask. An opaque plastic, cardboard, or acetate overlay for covering various areas of overhead transparencies; they are progressively lifted for disclosure.

Master. Material made or arranged for the purpose of reproducing additional copies.

Opaque. Materials that cannot be penetrated by light and cannot be projected on an overhead. Opaque shapes will project as silhouettes.

Overhead projector. A projector having a horizontal stage (aperture) and projecting a large image through a mirror and lens system onto a vertical screen behind the operator.

Overhead transparency. An image placed on acetate by hand, machine, or photographic methods and used on an overhead projector.

Overhead transparency mount. A frame for holding overhead transparency material for preservation, storage, and projection.

Overhead transparency hinge. An adhesive-backed Mylar material for attaching overlays and masks to mounted overhead transparencies.

Overlay. One or more transparent sheets containing additional information that is attached to the face of the mount and is progressively revealed by laying the overlays over the base cell.

Paste-up. Artwork, graphs, or lettering positioned onto a layout sheet and held in place with tape or rubber cement.

Realia. A term often used to represent any three-dimensional materials employed in instruction, such as rocks, leaves, and artifacts.

Register. Exact positioning of successive sheets of acetate to form a single composition through the use of precisely designed masters.

Squaring method. A method of enlarging, reducing, or distorting artwork by placing a grid over the original and copying the relative positions of the lines in each section onto a grid of another size.

Thermocopy machine. A machine using heat (infrared) lamps to actuate a dye coated onto acetate. This process is restricted to carbon-based artwork.

Thermocopy process. A reproduction process using an infrared lamp and an original or master having a carbon base to create an overhead transparency.

Transparency. *See* Overhead transparency.

Transparent. Materials that transmit light, can be seen through easily, and are capable of being projected on the overhead.

Transparent color tape. Pressure-sensitive acetate in tape form. Related to color adhesive. Comes in various colors, designs, and widths.

Appendix 2

Addresses of Materials Suppliers

Adhesive-Backed Color (Colored Adhesive)

Bourges Color Corp.
80 Fifth Avenue
New York, NY 10011

Chartpak Rotex
4 River Road
Leeds, MA 01053

3M Company
Visual Products Division
2501 Hudson Road
St. Paul, MN 55101

Art Supplies (General)

Arthur Brown & Bros.
2 West Forty-Sixth Street
New York, NY 10036

Dick Blick
P. O. Box 1267
Galesburg, IL 61401

Clip Artwork

A. A. Archibold Publishers
P. O. Box 57985
Los Angeles, CA 90057

Redi-Art Inc.
30 East Tenth Street
New York, NY 10003

Harry Volk Art Studio
Pleasantville, NJ 08232

Diazo

General Aniline & Film Corp.
140 West Fifty-First Street
New York, NY 10020

Dry-Transfer Lettering (Rub-On) and Texture Materials

Artype Inc.
345 East Terra Cotta Avenue
Crystal Lake, IL 60014

Chartpak Rotex
4 River Road
Leeds, MA 01053

Letraset Inc.
2379 Charleston Road
Mt. View, CA 94040

Prestype Corp.
194 Veterans Boulevard
Carlstadt, NJ 07072

Frames (Overhead Mounts)

The Holson Co.
Belden Avenue
Norwalk, CT 06897

Sherburn Graphic Products Inc.
P. O. Box 7503
Fort Worth, TX 76111

Heat Copy (Thermographic) Overhead Transparency Material

Columbia Ribbon & Carbon
    Manufacturing Co.
Glen Cove, NY 11542

3M Company
Visual Products Division
2501 Hudson Road
St. Paul, MN 55101

USI, Inc.
50 Maple Street
Branford Industrial Park
Branford, CT 06405

Polarizing Materials

Keuffel & Esser Co.
20 Whippany Road
Morristown, NJ 07960

Projection Optics
217 Eleventh Avenue
East Orange, NJ 07018

Technamation
30 Sagamore Hill Drive
Port Washington, NY 11505

Speedball Pens (Use with Acetate Ink)

Hunt Manufacturing Co.
1405 Locust Street
Philadelphia, PA 19102

Stencil Guides for Lettering

The C-Thru Ruler Co.
6 Britton Drive
Gloomfield, CT 06002

Koh-i-noor Rapidograph, Inc.
100 North Street
Bloomsburg, NJ 07110

Transparency Supplies (Pens, Acetate, Frames, etc.)

Audio Visual Communications, Inc.
159 Verdi Street
Farmingdale, NY 11735

Charles Besler Co.
219 South Eighteenth Street
East Orange, NJ 07018

Audio-visual products:
Lansford Publishing Co., Inc.
1088 Lincoln Avenue
P. O. Box 8711
San Jose, CA 95155 (Transp. Storage)

Transparency Tape (for Graphs)

ACS Tapes
217 California Street
Newton, MA 02158

Chartpak Rotex
4 River Road
Leeds, MA 01053

Micro-Tape
7005 Tujuanga Avenue
North Hollywood, CA 91605

Prestype, Inc.
194 Veterans Boulevard
Carlstadt, NJ 07072

Bourges Color Corp.
80 Fifth Avenue
New York, NY 10011

Appendix 3

Bibliography

Bullough, Robert V., *Creating Instructional Materials*. 2nd ed. Columbus, OH: Charles E. Merrill Publishing Co., 1978.

Green, Lee. *Use Your Overhead*. Wheaton, IL: Victor Books, 1979.

Heinich, Roberts; Molenda, Michael; and Russell, James, *Instructional Media and the New Technologies of Instruction*, New York: John Wiley & Sons, Chapter 5, 1982.

Kemp, Jerrold E. *Planning and Producing Audiovisual Materials*. 3rd ed. New York: Thomas Y. Crowell, 1975.

Laybourne, Kit, and Cianciolo, Pauline, eds. *Doing the Media, A Portfolio of Activities, Ideas and Resources, New Revised Edition*, New York: McGraw-Hill Book Co., Chapter 18, 1978.

Leonard, William C. *Overhead Production Methods*. Dubuque, IA: Kendall/Hunt Publishing Co., 1976.

MacGregor, A. J. *Graphics Simplified*. Toronto, Canada: University of Toronto Press, 1979.

Minor, Ed. *Simplified Techniques for Preparing Visual Instructional Media*. New York: McGraw-Hill Book Co., 1962.

Minor, Ed, and Frye, Harvey R. *Techniques for Producing Visual Instructional Media*. 2nd ed. New York: McGraw-Hill Book Co., 1977.

Morlan, John E. *Preparation of Inexpensive Teaching Materials*. 2nd ed. San Francisco: Chandler Publishing Co., 1973.

Oates, Stanton C. *Audiovisual Equipment: Self-Instructional Manual*. 3rd ed. Dubuque, IA: William C. Brown Co., 1975.

Ring, Arthur E., and Shelley, William J. *Learning with the Overhead Projector*. San Francisco: Chandler Publishing Co., 1969.

Satterthwaite, Les. *Graphics: Skills, Media, and Materials: A Laboratory Manual*. Dubuque, IA: Kendall/Hunt, 1972.

Schultz, Morton J. *The Teacher and the Overhead Projector: A Treasury of Ideas, Uses, and Techniques*. Englewood Cliffs, NJ: Prentice-Hall, Inc., 1965.

A Teacher's Guide to Overhead Projection. Holyoke, MA: Technifax, 1969.

Weagley, Richard P. *Teaching with the Overhead Projector*. Philadelphia: Instructo Products Co., 1963.

Wyman, Raymond. *Mediaware: Selection, Operation, and Maintenance*. 2nd ed. Dubuque, IA: William C. Brown Co., 1976.

Overhead Masters

The 22 overhead masters included in this appendix may be used on the overhead projector for instructional purposes.

THERMOGRAPHIC PROCESS REQUIRES CARBON

1. BLACK PRINTER'S INK ————

2. BLACK INDIA INK ————

3. ELECTROSTATIC COPY ————

4. #2 SOFT LEAD PENCIL ————

5. REPRODUCING TYPEWRITER ————

ADVANTAGES
OF THE OVERHEAD

★ IMAGE MANIPULATION

★ EYE CONTACT

★ USE IN A LIGHTED ROOM

★ QUICK, LOW COST

★ EASE of OPERATION

DISADVANTAGES
OF THE OVERHEAD

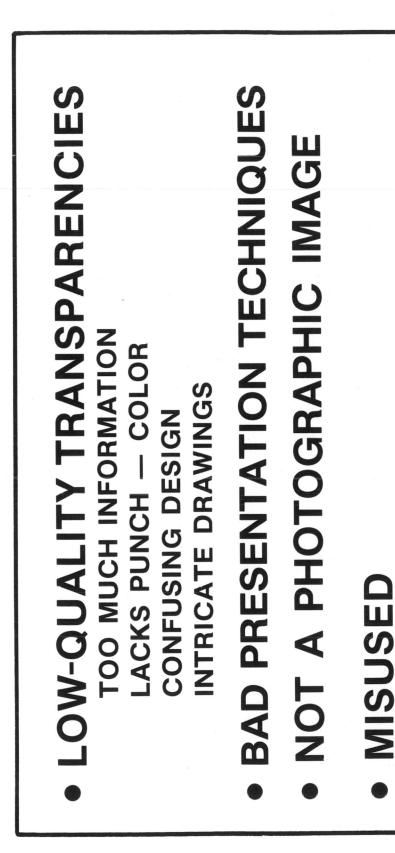

- **LOW-QUALITY TRANSPARENCIES**
  - TOO MUCH INFORMATION
  - LACKS PUNCH — COLOR
  - CONFUSING DESIGN
  - INTRICATE DRAWINGS
- **BAD PRESENTATION TECHNIQUES**
- **NOT A PHOTOGRAPHIC IMAGE**
- **MISUSED**

121

TYPES OF OVERHEAD MATERIALS

1 REALIA
REAL OBJECTS - IMAGE ENLARGEMENT
PLEXIGLAS OBJECTS - PROTRACTOR
CARDBOARD SHAPES

2 HANDMADE
TRACED
HAND-LETTERED

3 MACHINE MADE
COPY MACHINE
THERMOGRAPHIC
COLOR LIFT
DIAZO

4 PHOTOGRAPHIC
COPY CAMERA
ENLARGER

10 TASKS OVERHEAD DOES WELL

SPACIAL (maps) RELATIONSHIPS	IMAGE COMPARISON
TEMPORAL (time line) RELATIONSHIPS	REINFORCE MAIN POINTS
ORGANIZATIONAL (charts) RELATIONSHIPS	IMPORTANT SAYINGS
STATISTICAL (graphs) RELATIONSHIPS	PUPPETS
MECHANICAL WORKINGS (drawings)	GRAPHIC ENLARGEMENT

ADVANTAGES

OF MOUNTING TRANSPARENCIES

➤ AVOID LIGHT LEAK

➤ STIFF, EASIER TO STORE

➤ WRITE NOTES-QUESTIONS
ON MOUNTS

➤ CAN MOUNT:
OVERLAYS
MASK SYSTEMS

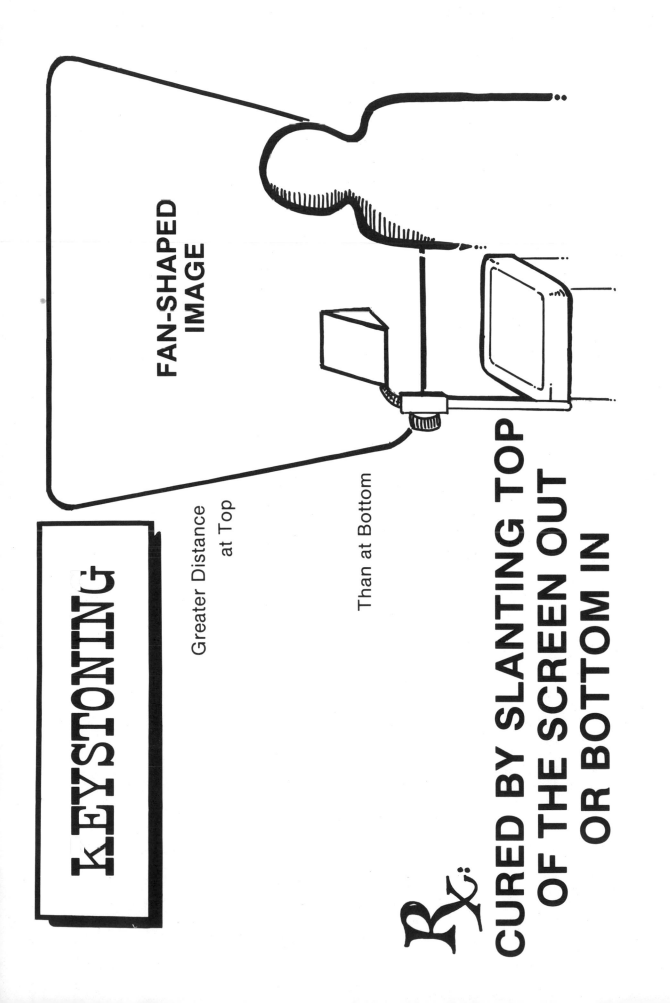

KEYSTONING

FAN-SHAPED IMAGE

Greater Distance at Top

Than at Bottom

Rx: CURED BY SLANTING TOP OF THE SCREEN OUT OR BOTTOM IN

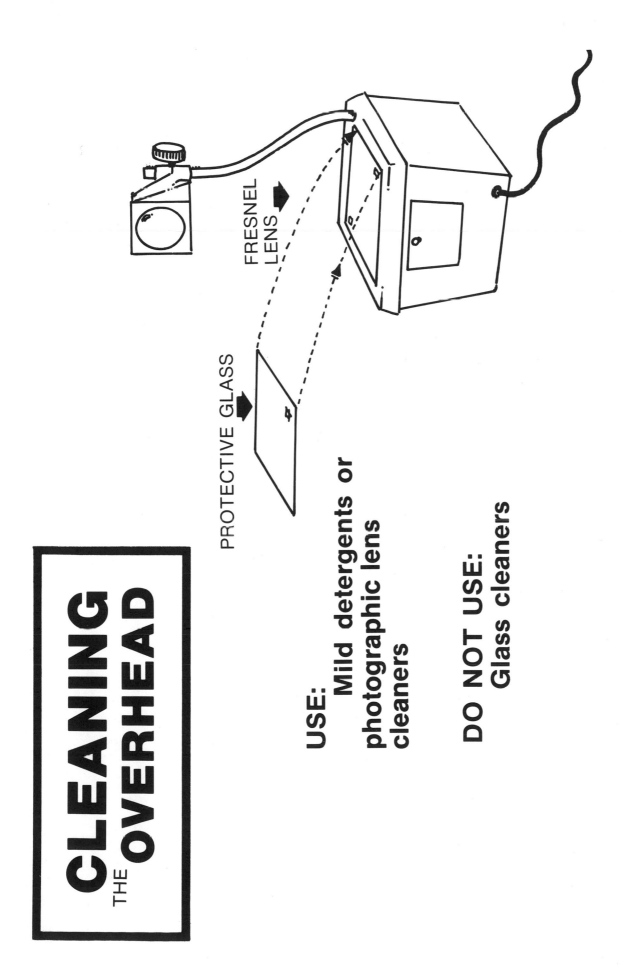

PROTECTIVE GLASS

FRESNEL LENS

CLEANING THE OVERHEAD

USE:
Mild detergents or photographic lens cleaners

DO NOT USE:
Glass cleaners

HAND-LETTERING TECHNIQUES

SHADOW

OUTLINE
USE DIFFERENT COLOR
FOR OUTLINE

REVERSAL

BAS RELIEF

HAND-LETTERING TECHNIQUES

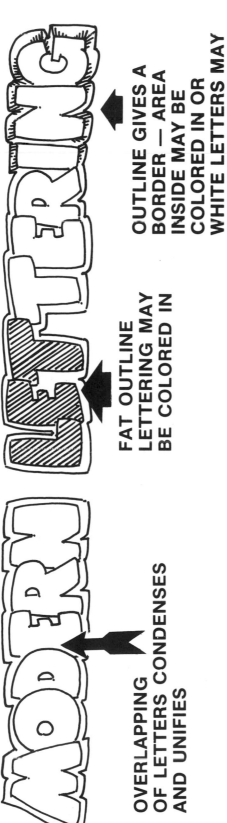

LETTERING

OUTLINE GIVES A BORDER — AREA INSIDE MAY BE COLORED IN OR WHITE LETTERS MAY BE USED ON A COLORED BACKGROUND

FAT OUTLINE LETTERING MAY BE COLORED IN

MODERN

OVERLAPPING OF LETTERS CONDENSES AND UNIFIES

IDEAS

BORDER MAY BE COLORED IN — USE TO HIGHLIGHT A WORD

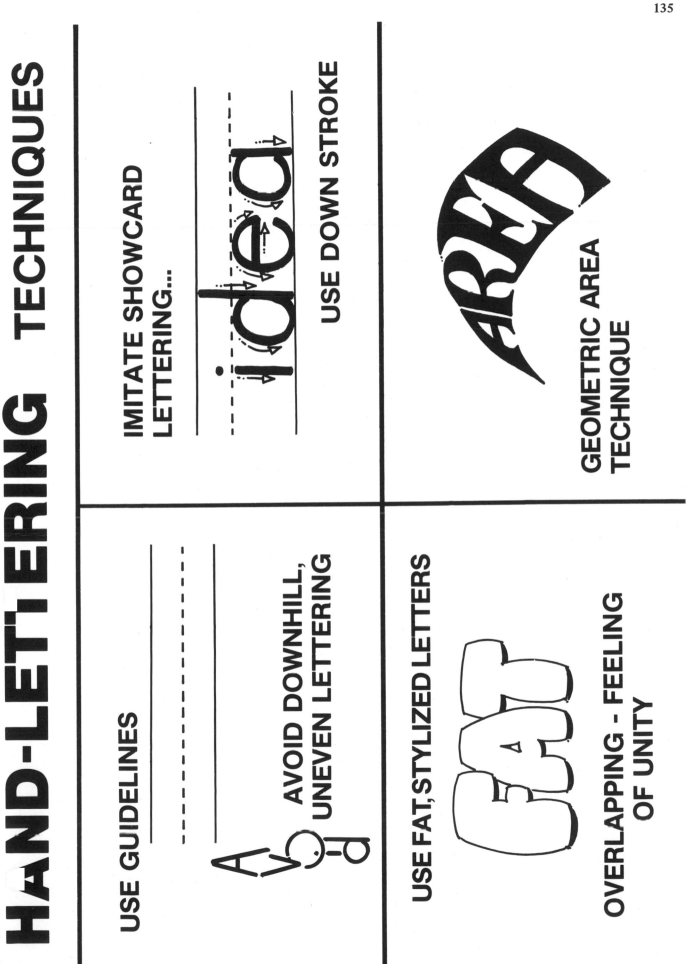

HAND-LETTERING TECHNIQUES

135

USE GUIDELINES

AVOID DOWNHILL, UNEVEN LETTERING

USE FAT, STYLIZED LETTERS

OVERLAPPING - FEELING OF UNITY

IMITATE SHOWCARD LETTERING...

idea

USE DOWN STROKE

GEOMETRIC AREA TECHNIQUE

MASK SYSTEMS

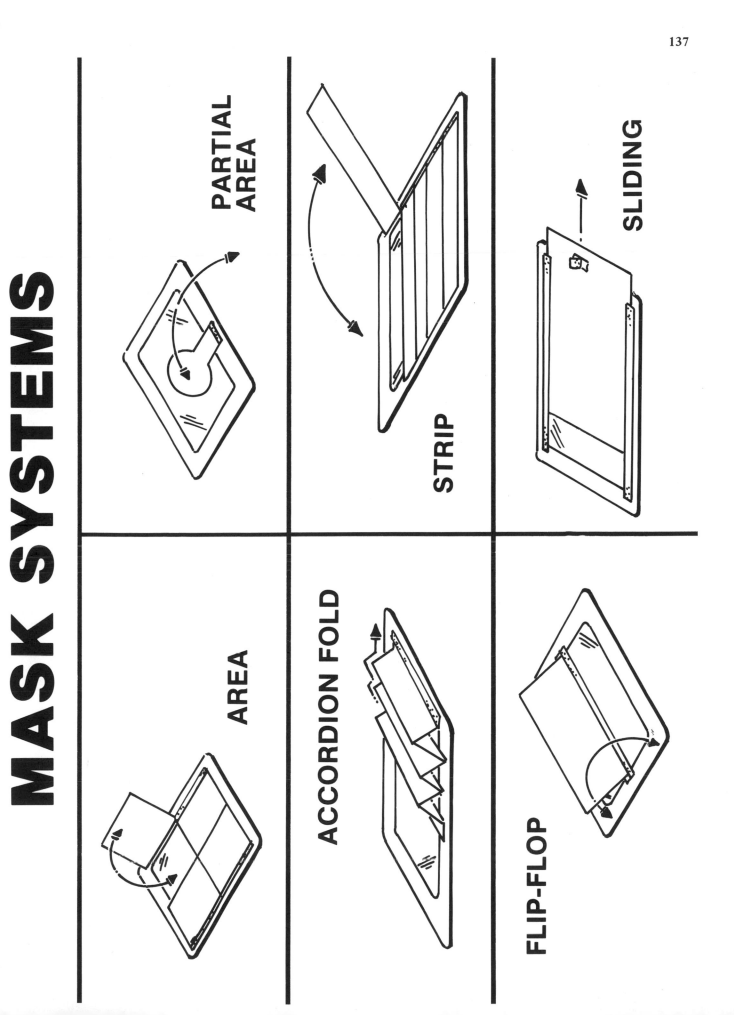

PARTIAL AREA

STRIP

SLIDING

AREA

ACCORDION FOLD

FLIP-FLOP

6 WAYS TO ADD COLOR

FELT PEN

ACETATE INK AND PEN

SHEETS or STRIPS of COLORED ACETATE

COLORED ADHESIVE MATERIAL

PACKET

COLORED LINE HEAT COPY

DIAZO FILM MATERIAL

STORING MOUNTED TRANSPARENCIES

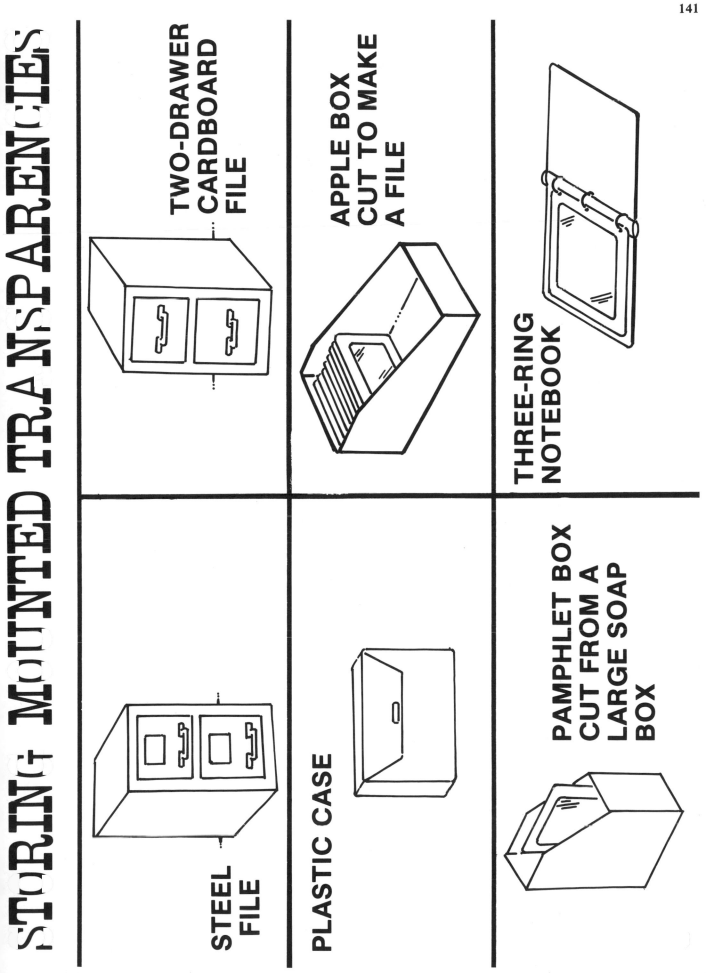

STEEL
FILE

TWO-DRAWER
CARDBOARD
FILE

PLASTIC CASE

APPLE BOX
CUT TO MAKE
A FILE

PAMPHLET BOX
CUT FROM A
LARGE SOAP
BOX

THREE-RING
NOTEBOOK

IDEAS FOR STORING UNMOUNTED TRANSPARENCIES

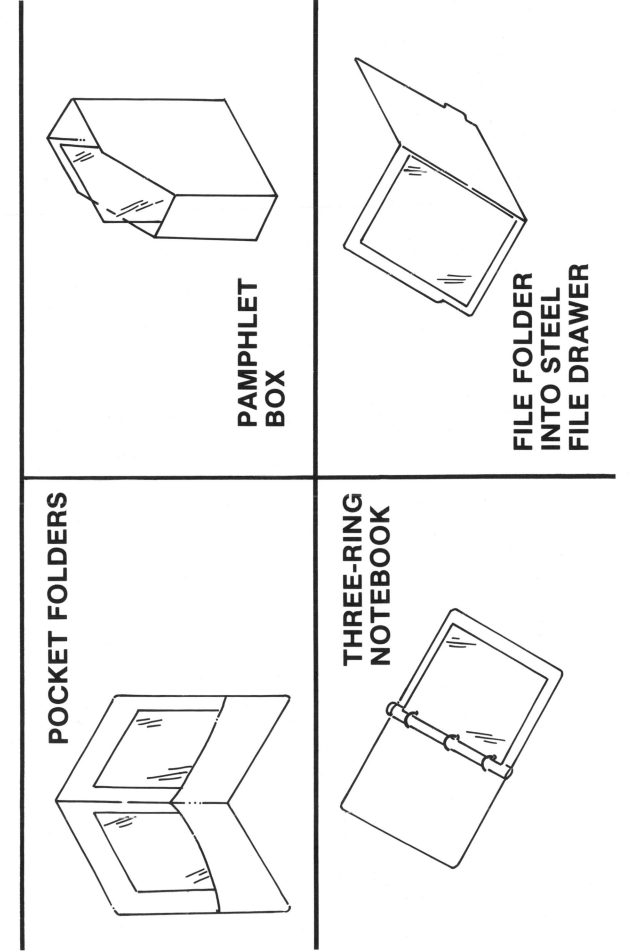

PAMPHLET BOX

FILE FOLDER INTO STEEL FILE DRAWER

POCKET FOLDERS

THREE-RING NOTEBOOK

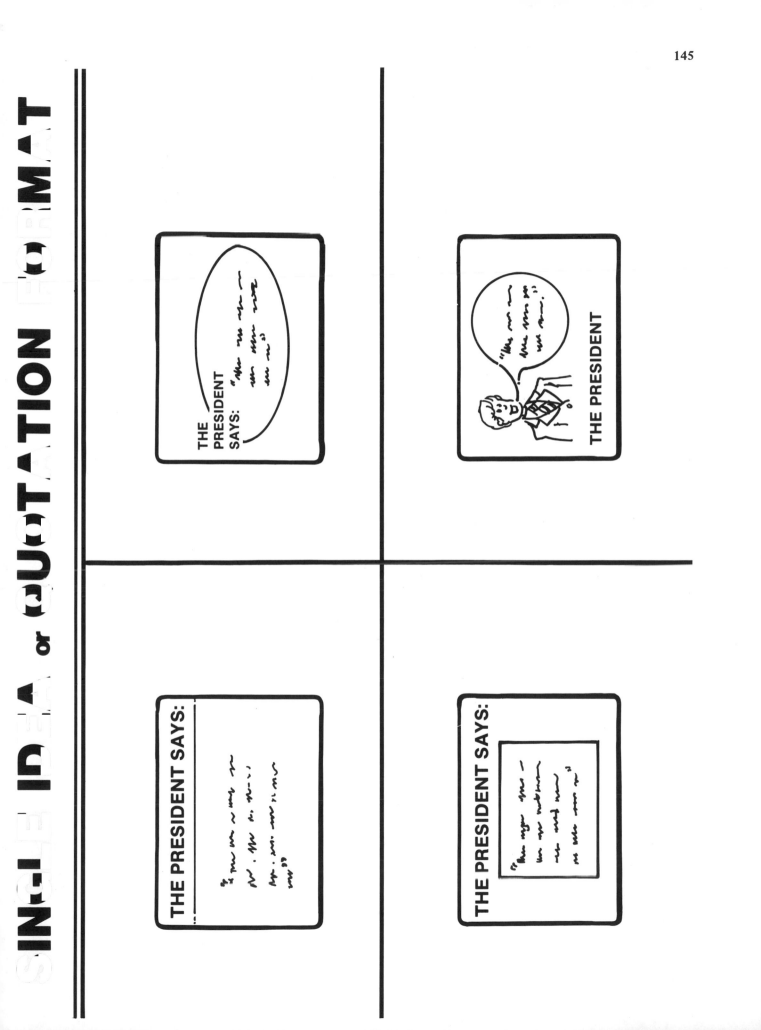

2 TYPES
OF HEAT COPY TRANSPARENCIES

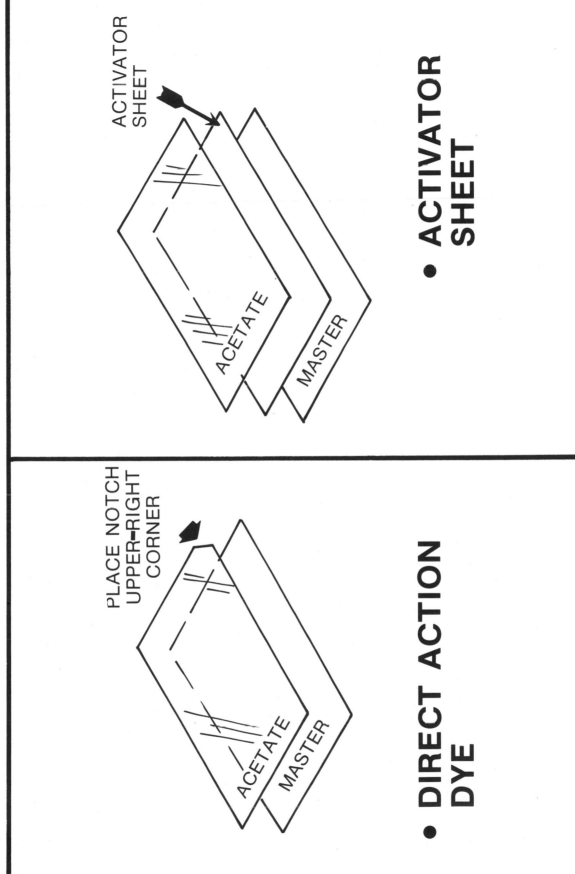

ACTIVATOR SHEET

ACETATE

MASTER

PLACE NOTCH UPPER-RIGHT CORNER

ACETATE

MASTER

- **ACTIVATOR SHEET**

- **DIRECT ACTION DYE**

RULE OF 6

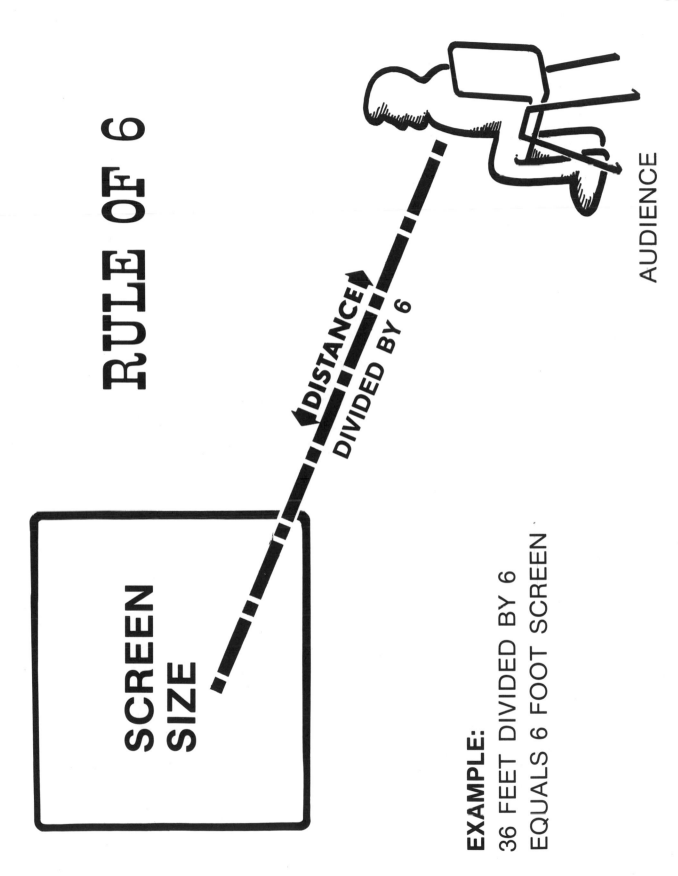

SCREEN SIZE

DISTANCE

DIVIDED BY 6

AUDIENCE

EXAMPLE:
36 FEET DIVIDED BY 6
EQUALS 6 FOOT SCREEN

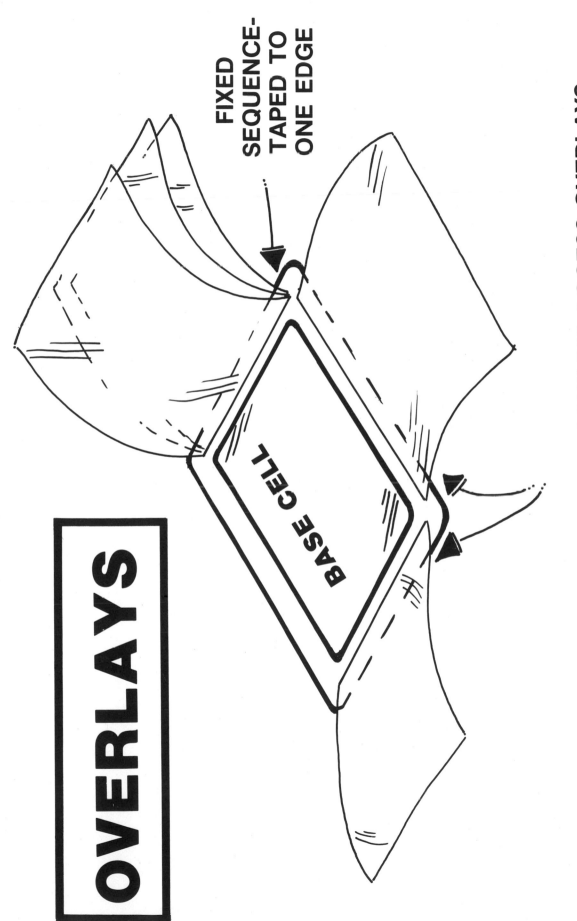

OVERLAYS

FIXED SEQUENCE-TAPED TO ONE EDGE

BASE CELL

RANDOM ACCESS-OVERLAYS TAPED TO DIFFERENT EDGES

MESSAGE DESIGN FORMATS

TWO POINTS
OR CONTRASTS

HEADING	
DO:	DON'T

THREE POINTS OR

HEADING	
One	Two	Three

HEADING	
Point One	
Point Two	
Point Three	

FOUR POINTS

HEADING	
Point One	Point Two
Point Three	Point Four

SIX POINTS

HEADING		
Point One	Point Two	
Point Three	Point Four	
Point Five	Point Six	

10 GUIDELINES

FOR MESSAGE DESIGN

1. One concept per transparency

2. Use a layout sheet

3. Use simple block lettering

4. Use line and geometric form

5. Use intersecting line for unity

6. Don't have more than 25-30 words

7. Avoid vertical lettering and composition

8. No more than 8-10 lines of type

9. No more than 6-8 words per line

10. Vary lettering size for emphasis

PARTS of a TRANSPARENCY

This is a
BASE CELL

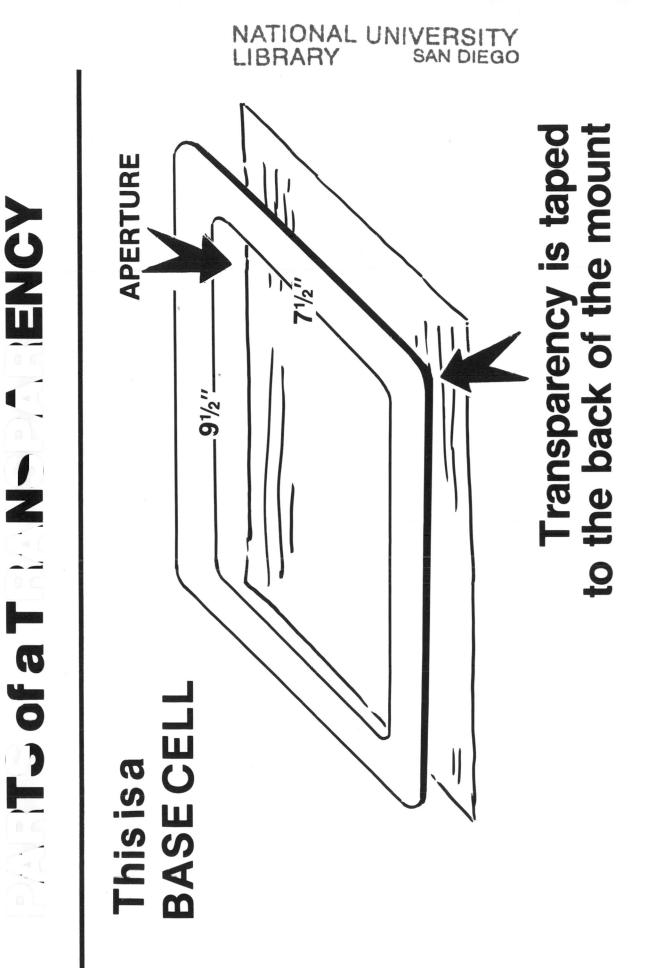

APERTURE

9½"

7½"

Transparency is taped
to the back of the mount